FROM MIST

AND STONE

FROM MIST AND STONE

THE HISTORY AND LORE OF THE CELTS AND VIKINGS

GEORGE W. STONE

NATIONAL GEOGRAPHIC

WASHINGTON, D.C.

CONTENTS

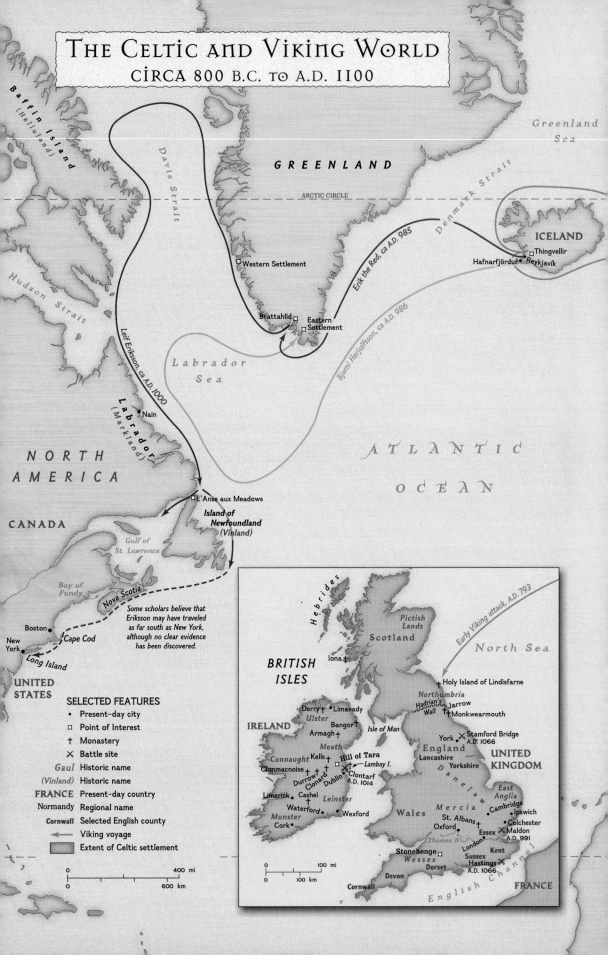

THE CELTIC AND VIKING WORLD
CIRCA 800 B.C. TO A.D. 1100

Baffin Island
(Helluland)

Davis Strait

GREENLAND

Greenland Sea

ARCTIC CIRCLE

Denmark Strait

ICELAND

□ Thingvellir
Hafnarfjördur □ ● Reykjavík

□ Western Settlement

Erik the Red, ca A.D. 985

Hudson Strait

Brattahlid ●
Eastern
□ Settlement

Bjarni Herjulfsson, ca A.D. 986

Labrador
Sea

Leif Eriksson, ca A.D. 1000

Labrador
(Markland)

● Nain

NORTH
AMERICA

ATLANTIC

OCEAN

CANADA

L'Anse aux Meadows □
Island of
Newfoundland
(Vinland)

Gulf of
St. Lawrence

Bay of
Fundy

Nova Scotia

Some scholars believe that
Eriksson may have traveled
as far south as New York,
although no clear evidence
has been discovered.

Boston ●

New ●
York

Cape Cod

Long Island

UNITED
STATES

SELECTED FEATURES

● Present-day city
□ Point of Interest
† Monastery
✕ Battle site
Gaul Historic name
(Vinland) Historic name
FRANCE Present-day country
Normandy Regional name
Cornwall Selected English county
→ Viking voyage
▨ Extent of Celtic settlement

0   400 mi
0   600 km

Hebrides

Pictish
Lands

BRITISH
ISLES

Scotland

Iona †

Early Viking attack, A.D. 793

North Sea

Holy Island of Lindisfarne †

Northumbria
Hadrian's † Jarrow
Wall † Monkwearmouth

Derry † ● Limavady
Ulster
Bangor †
Armagh †

Isle of Man

York ✕ Stamford Bridge
A.D. 1066

IRELAND

Meath

England

UNITED
KINGDOM

Connaught Kells †
Clonmacnoise †
Durrow † Clonard †
Dublin ●
Limerick ● Cashel ●
Waterford ●
Munster
Cork ●

Hill of Tara □
← Lambay I.
Clontarf
A.D. 1014

Leinster
● Wexford

Lancashire

Yorkshire

Danelaw

East
Anglia

Wales

Mercia

● Cambridge
St. Albans † ● Ipswich
Oxford ● Colchester
Essex ● Maldon
A.D. 991

London ●
Kent

Stonehenge ▲
Wessex Sussex Hastings ✕
Dorset A.D. 1066

Cornwall

Thames R.

FRANCE

English Channel

Devon

0   100 mi
0   100 km

Inset map (top right)

ENGLAND

London

✕ Hastings A.D. 1066

Thames

BELGIUM

GERMANY

English Channel

Normandy

Reims

Trier

Marne

Reinheim

Bohemia

Paris

Seine

Rhine

Moselle

Brittany
(Armorica)

Rennes

Vix □

✕ Alesia 52 B.C.

Salzburg □

Dürrnberg □

Hallstatt

Danube

Bourges

Burgundy

Hochdorf

La Tène □

FRANCE

*Lake
Neuchâtel*

SWITZ.

G A L S

Rhône

Liguria

Apennines

Po

Arles

Pisa

ITALY

0   200 mi

0   200 km

Marseille
(Massalia)

Telamon
225 B.C.

Tiber R.

Pyrenees

Rome

SPAIN

Mediterranean
Sea

Main map

A R C T I C

O C E A N

Norwegian Sea

ARCTIC CIRCLE

Earliest voyages
ca A.D. 860

Faroe Islands

NORWAY

SCANDINAVIA

SWEDEN

Bergen

Oslo

Uppsala

ca A.D. 800

Kaupang

Gokstad

Birka

Shetland
Islands

Area
enlarged
below, left

Orkney
Islands

Novgorod

R U S S I A

Volkhov

Hebrides

SCOTLAND

North Sea

Lindholm □

Volga

+ Lindisfarne

DENMARK

Skuldelev □

Western Dvina

York

Jutland

Hedeby

Baltic Sea

IRELAND

Dublin

ENGLAND

WALES

POLAND

London

Vistula

NETH.

GERMANY

BELG.

Kiev

Rhine

E U R O P E

Dnieper

Normandy

Paris

Danube

Hallstatt □

Volga

Area
enlarged
above, right

FRANCE

La Tène □

Carpathian Mountains

G A L S

Rhône

Po

BALKAN

Black Sea

Caspian Sea

Pyrenees

Marseille

ITALY

PENINSULA

Danube

IBERIAN

Rome

BULGARIA

Istanbul
(Constantinople, Byzantium)

SPAIN

MACEDONIA

PORTUGAL

PENINSULA

Mediterranean

GREECE

Galatia

TURKEY

ASIA MINOR

Andalusia

✕ Delphi
279 B.C.

Seville

Tigris

Euphrates

IRAN
(PERSIA)

Strait of Gibraltar

r a n e a n   S e a

Alexandria

A F R I C A

EGYPT

Nile

Red Sea

TROPIC OF CANCER

EDVVARD REX : VBI

ENIT : AD : EDVVARDV

CHAPTER 1

GREATNESS FOR ETERNITY

A Time of Gods and Heroes

Cattle die, kindred die,
Every man is mortal:
But I know one thing that never dies,
The glory of the great dead.
—"Hávamál: The Words of
Odin the High One"
from the POETIC EDDA

Irish Celts believed that the gods built the Poulnabrone dolmen in Burren, County Clare.

Gold cloak fastener, circa 700 B.C.

HIS IS THE STORY OF A GREAT CULTURAL EXCHANGE
spanning continents and centuries. It is about two civiliza-
tions that overlapped, intermingled, assimilated, traded,
battled, conquered, gained and lost kingdoms, explored
new lands, plundered, created, and destroyed. This story is, in short,
about the quest for immortality. Celts and Vikings both knew well that
enduring fame is not gained through divine favor alone but through
action—through the hard-won, cunningly conjured, battle-brave, semi-
mystical great deed. And even then, immortality is not conferred upon
an individual but upon an idea. Immortality, as the ancients would have
it, is a way not of escaping death but of overcoming it.

The idea of immortality seduced many great Celts and Vikings into
impossible challenges, and it goes far to explain their bravery in battle.
Men from both of these heroic cultures held a supremely egotistical pas-
sion for conquest, underscored by their willingness to die in pursuit of
greatness. They went beyond being merely willing to die for honor. They
constructed communities and cosmologies that rewarded them in death

*Perched spectacularly on a 300-foot cliff, semicircular ruins of the Dun Aengus ring fort on
Ireland's Aran Islands recall the harsh conditions of Bronze Age Celtic life.*

Celtic in origin and likely seized as booty by marauding Danes, the Gundestrup Cauldron was recovered from a Danish peat bog. It dates from the fourth or third century B.C.

for bravery in life. For these scourges and superachievers, benefactors and barbarians, the more spectacular the challenge, the greater the glory. For Celts, eternity was about the soul. If they achieved greatness, their souls would migrate to the next able warrior. For Vikings, eternity was physical. It meant sirenlike Valkyries and bottomless bumpers of mead in the Heroes' Hall at Valhalla. Their quests for immortality explain both their monumental accomplishments and their limb-smashing defeats.

FROM CENTRAL EUROPE, from about the eighth to the first century B.C., the warrior-farmers known as Celts spread into Italy, France (or Gaul), Greece, the Balkans, Asia Minor, Spain, Britain, and Ireland. Far from being backwater pagans, as they were cast by Mediterranean civilizations, the Celts were culturally and economically transactional people. They established an active economy based on broad trade routes; they created Europe's first major industrial revolution, first common market, first court of arbitration; and they held highly evolved scientific and religious ideas.

"Celts introduced soap to the Greeks and Romans, invented chain armor, were first to shoe horses and give shape to handsaws, chisels, files, and other tools we use today," notes NATIONAL GEOGRAPHIC magazine writer Merle Severy. "They developed seamless iron rims for their wheels; set our standard 4-foot, 8.5-inch railroad gauge with the span of their chariots; pioneered the iron plowshare, the rotary flour mill, a wheeled harvester; ... and secured women's rights centuries before late bloomers began to roast male chauvinist pigs." And, most enduringly, the Celts made verses in their lyrical, mystical language, sung by bards to celebrate their ancient heroes and gods.

VIKING SOCIETY WAS MORE CLOSED than that of the Celts, more fixated on battle and material acquisition, yet it brought more to the world than just terror. Devastating raids in the late eighth and ninth centuries formed a reputation for piracy and destruction, but in many ways Viking culture was as sophisticated as those they ravaged.

The defining mark of Viking success was mobility. Their ingenious ships not only provided an element of surprise necessary for raiding but also carried them into the far reaches of the known world. Danish Viking ships raided southward to the Mediterranean and eastward into Germany. Swedish Vikings reached towns along rivers in eastern Europe and gained control of the key trade routes between the Baltic and Black Seas. They settled Kiev and Novgorod, lending their tribal name, *Rus,* to the land still called Russia. And when not plundering, Norwegian Vikings moved westward, colonizing Iceland and Greenland. Leif Eriksson, a Viking explorer, landed in North America about 500 years before Christopher Columbus. As a result of the Viking migrations, modern civilization enjoys two treasures: a system of representative government, or parliament, developed from the Althing, or Great Assembly, that first convened in Thingvellir, Iceland, in A.D. 930. The Vikings' sagas and *eddas,* stories and poems, still ring with epic excitement and lyrical meaning today.

"In Iceland, the age of the Vikings is also called the Saga Age," writes Robert Kellogg, an expert in Norse literature. Kellogg points out about 40 works of medieval Icelandic literature that he considers "fictionalized accounts of events that took place in Iceland" during the era of the Vikings.

"The settlement of Iceland, which began about 870, was part of a larger movement of Norse expansion," Kellogg explains. The earliest settlers came from the west coast of Norway, but "a significant number came from Norse communities in Ireland and Great Britain, bringing people of Celtic origin with them.... By 1000 a new cultural phase was under way." Many Norsemen were converting to Christianity, which not only slowed down their raids on churches but also introduced "monasticism, literacy and the internationalist perspective of the church hierarchy" into Norse culture and "laid the foundation for a post-Viking educational system"—a system that depended on reading books.

"Literacy made possible the conversion of rich ancient Viking oral traditions of myth and legend into written literature, as was also happening in Celtic Britain," Kellogg continues, "the crowning achievement of medieval narrative art in Scandinavia." Written in "straightforward, clear prose rather than verse," Viking sagas recount tales not about "kings and princes and semi-divine heroes but about wealthy and powerful farmers."

THE PEAK OF VIKING PROWESS came hundreds of years after the Celts achieved their greatest successes, and long before either was established as a society, indigenous peoples inhabited their lands. Ancient standing stones and stone circles such as Stonehenge have long been associated with the Druids, the Celtic class of priests, but the megaliths typically predate the Celts by at least a thousand years. The priests of megalithic times may have influenced the Druids' religion and science, but to the agricultural Celts the great stone temples were so foreign as to be interpreted not as the work of man but as natural shrines of the spirits. As they did with springs and groves, so the Celts viewed megaliths like Stonehenge with awe. They produced legends about the origins and purposes of the megaliths.

To the Celts, the Earth—along with its rocks, rivers, bogs, springs, and mountains—was alive and divine. They saw megalithic structures—altars, rings, and stone circles—as portals to the otherworld. In Ireland these portals, called dolmens, consist of three to seven upright stones bearing a massive capstone. These gigantic stone tables, likely intended as above-ground grave sites, were so imposing that the Irish Celts attributed their construction to the gods. "When the Celts came to Ireland they found many such structures, originally the inner chambers of Stone Age tombs and perhaps already more than 1,000 years old," explains Juliette Wood,

The winter solstice sun illuminates spiral motifs at Newgrange, an Irish megalith dating from about 3000 B.C. Celts believed the site was a sidhe, or fairy mound, a dwelling place of gods.

author of *The Celts: Life, Myth, and Art.* "Irish myth tells of a divine race, the Tuatha Dé Danann (Children of the Goddess Danu) who retreated through these stone portals following the invasion of the Gaels and founded a new kingdom in the parallel cosmos. Known in Irish as *sidhe,* or fairy mounds, these entrances to the Otherworld ... were also once revered as the 'hostels' of individual gods and goddesses."

Dolmens exist in great numbers from Scandinavia through Europe to the Strait of Gibraltar, around the Mediterranean, and far beyond, but the megaliths of the British Isles remain the most magical and mythical. The temple of Stonehenge, a complex of 56 standing stones in south-central England, was built in three stages between 3200 B.C. and 1500 B.C. Whoever the ancient people were who contributed to the construction of Stonehenge, they preceded the Celts by a thousand years.

ABOVE: *Found in a tomb in Strettweg, Austria, this Celtic bronze wagon from the seventh century B.C. may depict a fertility rite presided over by a goddesss. The blood of the sacrificed stag, spilled to the ground and absorbed into the soil, ensures prosperity.*

LEFT: *An early Scandinavian boat carving decorates a rock found near Frederickstad, Norway.*

Ireland's hill of Tara is an emerald vista dotted with a network of man-made burial mounds, earthworks, and monumental stones. Distinctive features on Tara's crest date to 2500 B.C. For Celts across centuries this hill has been the most sacred place on Earth, the site of mythic events, coronations, and festivals. But Tara and other venerated sites were largely abandoned following a massive volcanic eruption in Iceland in about 1050 B.C., which sent plumes of ash over Britain and Ireland, causing a collapse in agriculture. Existing cultures and their secrets disappeared. When Iron Age Celtic societies moved into these areas, they resurrected their forebears as the legendary gods and heroes of their mythology. Ancient sites became dwelling places, trysting places, and destinations for pilgrimages and festivals, some of which form the foundations of celebrations observed today.

Encased in clay that has served as a preservative, the countless fragments of the

Oseberg Viking burial ship were uncovered in 1904 in a fjord near Oslo, Norway. ❋

Druidic tradition is recalled across Europe and America on May Day, honoring springtime's mystical renewal. Modern celebrations feature pagan traditions such as dancing around maypoles—totems of fertility—and setting bonfires—sacrifices to the gods or efforts to frighten away evil spirits. Halloween, bookend to May Day, began in the Celtic festival of Samhain (pronounced SOW-in), which marked the end of summer's harvest and the beginning of the dark, cold winter, a time associated with death as well. Celts believed that on this eve of their new year, the boundary blurred between the worlds of the living and the dead. They observed Samhain on the night of October 31, when the ghosts of the dead returned, causing trouble and damaging crops but opening a spiritual portal that enabled predictions about the future.

Other British earthworks recall the Celtic days of yore. Monumental carvings in chalk soil—notably the 374-foot-long White Horse of Uffington near Oxford and the 200-foot-tall club-bearing Cerne Giant

The Swedish island Bjorko (Birch) became a major trading center for Vikings, Russians, and Arabs. Its settlement, Birka, peaked between A.D. 800 and 975, placing it among Sweden's oldest cities.

in Dorset—reveal a Celtic flair for abstract forms. Radiant white horses were important to the Celts. Gods and goddesses were believed to take on equine form, and horses were sometimes sacrificed in their honor. The Iron Age Cerne Giant "is both hostile and benign, remote, lofty, watchful, on his tranquil terrain," writes Anne Ross in *A Traveller's Guide to Celtic Britain*. He is an "ancestral god in the shape of this great vigourous Giant, a skilled warrior, menacing, comforting, timeless, enduring."

THE FIRST INDO-EUROPEAN PEOPLE to spread across Europe, the Celts created Europe's first civilization north of the Alps. They advanced in waves, east as far as the Black Sea and Asia Minor, southwest into Spain and central Italy, and west to the British Isles. The main migration was by the

Galli, or Gauls, into France, northern Italy, and the north of Europe. Between the seventh and fifth centuries B.C., two early concentrations of settlement were established, one in the western Alps and another south of the upper Danube. By 400 B.C. the Celts had settled in Spain and the British Isles, over virtually all of what is now France, and then in modern Italy's Po Valley and Liguria. They trounced a Roman army on the Tiber in 396 B.C. and soon after laid waste to much of Rome and its capitol. To the east they moved down the Danube. Soon after 300 B.C. the Macedonians suffered their depredations. The Celts raided Delphi in Greece and some even crossed into Asia Minor, settling in Galatia, or what is now Turkey.

A wealth of information about the early Celts comes from ancient Greek and Roman writers who, due to Mediterranean elitism and cultural supremacy, tended to lump together the vast range of Celtic tribes and summarily dismiss them all as barbaric. The Greek geographer Strabo, a keen observer who wrote a 17-volume description of Europe, Asia, Egypt, and Libya, held a slight distaste for the boastful Celts, whom he called "war-mad," "high-spirited," and "quick for battle although otherwise simple and not uncouth." The Celts, he wrote, "are willing to risk everything they have with nothing to rely on other than their sheer physical strength and courage. If gentle persuasion is used, however, they will readily apply themselves to useful things such as education and the art of speaking. Their strength is due partly to their size—for they are large—and partly to their numbers." Strabo also noted their "propensity for empty-headed boasting" and their fondness for jewelry. "They wear a lot of gold," he reported, and "put golden collars around their necks and bracelets on their arms and wrists, while dignitaries wear dyed or stained clothing that is spangled with gold. Their vanity therefore makes them unbearable in victory, while defeat plunges them into deepest despair."

Absorbed into the Roman Empire as Britons, Gauls, Boii, Galatians, and Celtiberians, the Celts did not truly submit to any will but their own. Stubborn individuality ranks high among their virtues. By the end of the second century B.C., Mediterranean Gaul was a Roman colony. Julius Caesar led a series of campaigns north via the Rhône Valley, stretching Roman control to the English Channel and integrating the most economically advanced areas of the barbarian world (as the Romans saw it) into their empire. The Celts were "bad citizens, but good mercenaries and excellent subjects," writes Theodor Mommsen, the Nobel Prize–winning historian. "The Celts shook the foundations of all the states of Antiquity, but they founded none of lasting importance." Only in Ireland, Scotland, Wales, southwest England, and Brittany did the Celtic sensibility survive.

A two-faced statue reminiscent of the Roman god Janus suggests that a druidic cult existed on County Fermanagh's Boa Island long after Christianity reached Ireland.

Ireland, settled by Iberian and Briton Celts, staged a thrilling Celtic renaissance in the early Middle Ages with the creation of such illuminated masterpieces as the *Book of Kells* and the *Lindisfarne Gospels*.

Celtic efforts to establish political entities, however, "belong among the greatest failures in the history of ancient Europe," historian Raymond Lantier believes. "Their adventure ... reflects the nature of a people, born

A stylized horse pulls a golden sun in this bronze votive offering dating from about 1400 B.C. Discovered in Trundholm, Norway, the object likely played a part in a fertility ritual.

rebels against any rigid order, who could never manage to attain the concept of a state. And yet the Celts played a great part in history." For Lantier, "of what survives of the Celts, their sculptures and decorative art are still today the most eloquent and vivid evidence of the culture which united this restless people." Treasures like torques—golden neck rings that symbolized the cycle of life, death, and rebirth—and the magnificent Gundestrup Cauldron—a large, multipaneled silver vessel excavated in Denmark—best tell the story of how the Celts dominated Europe for 500 years, valuing glory and wit, wine and gold, and spending their lives in an unquenchable quest for greatness.

THE HISTORY OF THE CELTS SPANS MILLENNIA; that of the Viking conquest spans roughly 250 years, but in that quarter-millennium the Norsemen transformed Europe, penetrated Asia, and explored America. The Viking age is usually said to begin in June 793, when Norwegians attacked Lindisfarne (Holy Island) on England's northeast coast. Earlier raids, including one in 789 on the Dorset coast, hinted at the doom destined for the British Isles, but the butchery at Lindisfarne signaled the presence of a permanent new threat. A wave of Norwegian raids against

England, Ireland, the Isle of Man, and Scotland soon followed. Ireland's 12th-century saga, *Cogadh Gaedhel re Gallaibh (The War of the Irish with the Foreigners)*, describes the terror that the Vikings delivered: "Although there were an hundred hard-steeled iron heads on one neck, and an hundred sharp, ready, never-rusting brazen tongues in every head, and an hundred garrulous, loud, unceasing voices from every tongue, they could not recount or narrate or enumerate, or tell, what all the Gaedhel [people of Ireland] suffered in common, both men and women, laity and clergy, old and young, noble and ignoble, of hardship, and of injury, and of oppression, in every house, from these valiant, wrathful, foreign, purely pagan people."

Known for their seamanship and their ruthlessness, Viking warriors carried spears and axes, bows and arrows. The richest among them carried long double-edged iron swords. A Viking broad ax had a long handle and a large flat blade with a curved, razor-sharp cutting edge, swung with a chopping or hacking motion at an opponent's arms or legs. Warriors carried round wooden shields. If they wore armor, it was made from thick layers of animal hides, sometimes with bone sewn in for added protection. Fighters wore cone-shaped helmets made of leather, and leaders wore metal helmets and coats of mail. Despite the stereotype, Viking helmets never had horns. Such an extravagance was more in keeping with the Celts, whose sartorial sensibility might have favored raven feathers, boar tusks, or deer antlers atop a helmet, not cattle horns.

The Viking longship, a deadly vessel, gave sailors a considerable advantage in their early raids. They could plunder and run before opposing troops could gather to resist them. Viking victories were inconceivable without their sleek, fast, flexible, serpent- or dragon-headed vessels. Two amazing such Viking ships were discovered in Norway in modern times: Excavations of the Gokstad ship in 1880 and the Oseberg ship in 1904 launched the great age of Viking archaeology. The 70-foot Oseberg ship, built before A.D. 820 and buried ceremonially in 850, contained the bodies of two women, a wagon and four sleighs, a tent, cooking utensils, tools for textile production, chests and small boxes for valuables, cooking utensils, shovels and rakes, a saddle, a dog collar, and more. The Gokstad ship, constructed in the 850s and buried in about 880, is typical of the vessels used in early Viking attacks. Both ships and their treasures are displayed at Oslo's Viking Ship Museum.

Fertile farms, rich churches, and well-stocked monasteries made Ireland an attractive target. By plundering, the Vikings may have destroyed Ireland's chance for cultural leadership in Europe, but they did establish the island's first genuine cities: Limerick, Cork, Wexford, Waterford, and Dublin. Political disarray in early ninth-century Europe gave the Vikings more opportunities they couldn't refuse. Norwegian raiders looted and burned

❈ King Arthur ❈

A Celtic King

WHETHER KING ARTHUR EVER REALLY EXISTED IS BY NOW a mere technicality. The Arthurian and Grail legends are by far the Celts' greatest contribution to world literature. The essential legend introduces Arthur as a leader of unimpeachable honor who defeats the Saxons and other enemies and unites the people of Britain in peace and harmony. More elaborate retellings portray Arthur, born to be king, answering the wizard Merlin's spell by pulling the sword Excalibur from a rock. Arthur rules in Camelot and meets, courts, and marries the beautiful Guinevere. He founds a fellowship of knights known as the society of the Round Table. Eventually most of Arthur's knights embark on the greatest quest of all, in search of the Holy Grail, the chalice used by Jesus at the Last Supper. The Round Table finally disbands, signaling the end of Camelot. Arthur's kingdom weakens from within, partly due to the illicit love between Queen Guinevere and the French knight Lancelot. Arthur is struck down by his own illegitimate son, Mordred. He retreats to Avalon to recover, pledging to return in the hour of Britain's greatest need.

If Arthur was a historical figure, he was a commander who defeated the Saxons at Mount Badon in A.D. 516 and died at Camlan in 537, according to Nennius, a ninth-century historian. His legend emerged in the chaotic twilight of Rome-dominated Britain. In the years following the end of centralized Roman rule in 410, the country split into feuding kingdoms. Saxon attacks through 450 pushed the Celtic Britons into Wales and Cornwall. They needed a powerful leader, and in Arthur they may have found one. His rule would have coincided with a long stalemate with the Saxons.

The Arthurian legend first arose in a Welsh heroic poem that named his court not Camelot but Celliwig, in Cornwall, southwest England. The rugged north coast of Tintagel (Dún Tagell to the Celts) was part of the Dumnonia kingdom, stronghold of a Celtic king. Ruins at Tintagel date to 700 years after Arthur's time, yet the site swells with legend and lore. Geoffrey of Monmouth, a 12th-century Welsh cleric whose *Historia*

Regum Brittaniae (*History of the Kings of Britain*) combined history, legend, and artistic license, cast Arthur as the ultimate chivalric hero. Geoffrey's Arthur fights giants and dragons, invades France, and even defeats the Roman emperor. Within a century, Geoffrey's history had fired the imagination of writers across Europe. Each added a new wrinkle to the tale of King Arthur. The entire colorful rise and fall of Arthur and his world was narrated in verse by the English poet Sir Thomas Malory in *Le Morte d'Arthur*, written in the mid-1400s and published in 1485.

Perhaps the most surprising Arthurian rebirth is Mark Twain's *A Connecticut Yankee in King Arthur's Court*, in which a 19th-century American travels back to Arthur's time. The Connecticut Yankee has just the right American know-how to be a success in chivalric times. Merlin proves a charlatan, but Arthur is portrayed as kind, gentle, and a bit simple-minded—just like his realm. Evil existed, but honor and chivalry always prevailed—exactly how life should be, at least in legend.

King Arthur was sometimes encircled, sometimes entrapped, by his valiant, courtly, and potentially unruly Knights of the Round Table, as shown in this 1634 engraving.

towns in France, Italy, and Spain; Danish Vikings attacked Belgium, France, and the Netherlands. In 865, the Danes invaded England, conquering all its kingdoms but Wessex and settling in the eastern half of the country. They eventually withdrew eastward, concentrating in an area that became known as the Danelaw. When Danish Vikings later laid siege to Paris, the French king bought them off with the land now called Normandy, Land of the Northmen.

In about A.D. 870 Norwegian Vikings began to migrate to Iceland. By the mid-900s their population numbered about 25,000. As the Norwegians explored the North Atlantic—paving the way for Leif Eriksson to ply the coast of Nova Scotia, possibly reaching as far south as Cape Cod in A.D. 1000—other Vikings raided Spain and Mediterranean ports, developing permanent settlements in western Europe from which assaults could begin earlier in the year. Swedish Vikings forged profitable trade routes in eastern Europe that extended to Byzantium, Persia, and even India. The incorrigible Danes attacked England again and ruled the land from 1016 to 1042. The Viking age didn't conclude until the death of the last great Viking hero, Harald Hardraada, King of Norway, at the Battle of Stamford Bridge, leading to the Norman conquest of England in 1066.

BUT THERE IS MORE TO THE STORY of the Celts and the Vikings than the dates and geographic range of their conquests. How did these cultures develop, interact, and launch their campaigns for immortality? If chance were to provide a motive and venue for the fearsome Northmen to meet the Celtic Irish on the battlefield, who would arise victorious? The Battle of Clontarf, in 1014, was just such an event, and its surprising outcome shaped the destinies of two of history's greatest warrior cultures. By the end of "a battle bloody, furious, red, valiant, heroic, manly, rough, cruel, and heartless," a victorious king lay dead and a vanquished foe was flushed from a yew tree. The "glory of the great dead" was everywhere apparent—as was the gore of the great dead. All that remained after the conflict was to sort the bodies, to determine which souls would transmigrate to other brave Celts and which warriors were bound for Valhalla. But to reach full understanding of this battle's grand conclusion, we must step back almost 2,000 years, to the mythical mist and stone that gave rise to two of Europe's most commanding civilizations.

Stonehenge was constructed in three stages, from 3200 to 1500 B.C., corresponding to the development of ancient Britain. A large earth rampart, or henge, forms the site's foundation.

The Uffington Horse—dating from 1000 B.C., late Bronze Age, the oldest hill figure

in Britain—likely represents Epona, a goddess worshipped throughout the Celtic world. ❋

CHAPTER 2

THE CELTS
Mystical Conquerors of Ancient Europe

*We reached the deep-flowing
ocean where the Cimmerians
have their lands and their town.
This people is hidden under
clouds, in mists that the sun's
bright rays have never pierced…
a dismal night hangs over
these unfortunates.*
—HOMER, THE ODYSSEY,
BOOK XI

Mistletoe, sacred to the Celts, was believed to provide a magical cure for barrenness.

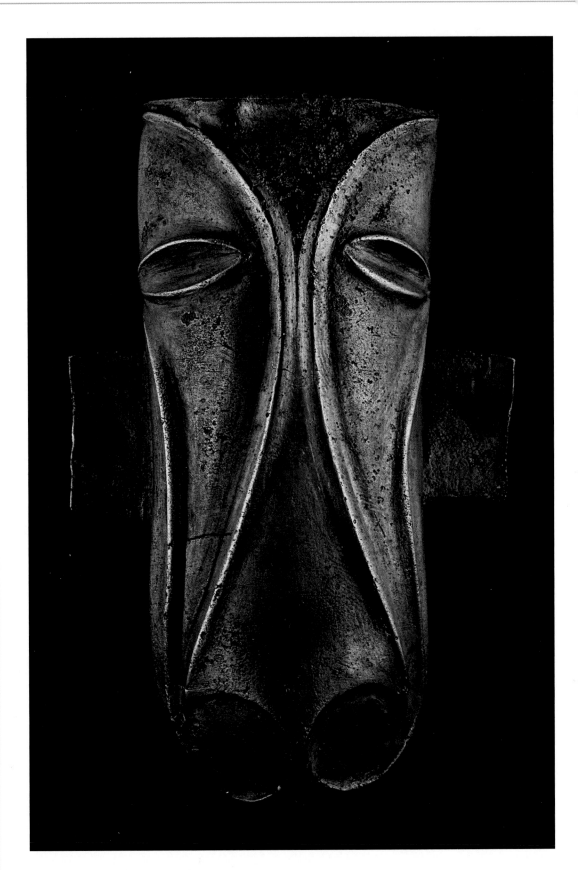

La Tène vase from France, circa 400-350 B.C.

 HEN HOMER MADE THIS MENTION OF THE CELTS (AS THE Cimmerians) in the eighth or ninth century B.C., he was not alone in imagining that these rustic northerners may have emerged from the shadows. Homer was Greek, after all, and he believed that his culture was responsible for all that was worth knowing in the world. The Greeks had invented drama and philosophy; they were mathematicians, poets, warriors, and seamen without equals. The Celts, on the other hand, were a loosely affiliated band of central European tribes living off the land. Not much was known of these Paleolithic wanderers, who began to populate the continent around 10,000 B.C. and emerged as a culture in the first millennium B.C. Whatever was known, Homer summarized in a few choice words—perhaps the first written record of the Celts. Hidden under clouds, behind the mists, beneath a dismal night: These strange hunter-gatherers were, in the eyes of the Mediterranean world, the newts of the north country.

But if the Celts were troubled by the perpetual disparagements cast upon them by their more civilized neighbors, they never let on. Or

Essential to Celtic expansion, horses served both utilitarian and sacred roles.
This four-inch sheet bronze ornament mask was found in Stanwick, England.

perhaps it's better to say that they got their revenge. This group of related tribes, linked by language, religion, and culture, gradually became farmers, then sophisticated metalworkers, and eventually gave rise to the first civilization north of the Alps.

To Bronze Age northern Europe, the Celts introduced the use of iron for tools and weapons. That innovation—along with their fierceness as warriors—gave them dominance in the sixth century B.C. over a region that stretched from southern Germany, around the source of the Danube, to the Iberian Peninsula, today's Spain and Portugal. By the fifth century B.C. some Celts had amassed great wealth by controlling trade routes along the Danube, Rhine, Rhône, and Seine Rivers, waterways that enabled vast migration into eastern Europe. And in the fourth century B.C., the Celts overran northern Italy, Macedonia, and Thessaly. They caught the eye of Greek historian Herodotus, who mentioned these

ABOVE: *Roman Emperor Hadrian came to Britannia in* A.D. *122, brought by news of Celtic rebellions in northern England.*

LEFT: *Hadrian withdrew his troops from northern England and began construction of an enormous wall. It stretched 76 Roman miles, from the Irish Sea to the North Sea, and successfully blocked the northern Celts from entering and raiding Roman Britannia.*

pioneering Europeans in a passage comparing the Ister (Danube) and the Nile: "The river Ister rises among the Celts and the town of Pyrene and crosses the whole of Europe. And the Celts are beyond the Pillars of Hercules [two promontories on the eastern end of the Strait of Gibraltar], next to the Cynesii, who live furthest west of all the peoples of Europe." A fifth century B.C. wave of Celtic expansion coincided with the Golden Age of Greece and increased the Greeks' known world considerably.

THE NAME CELT FIRST APPEARS IN THE GREEK as *Keltoi,* a term used by classical writers to describe a race of warrior tribes from north of the Alps, an exotic and unruly people who raged into battle aboard fast two-horse chariots, screaming and naked, creating terror, confusion, and the letting of blood with their large iron hacking swords and sharp spears. These effective

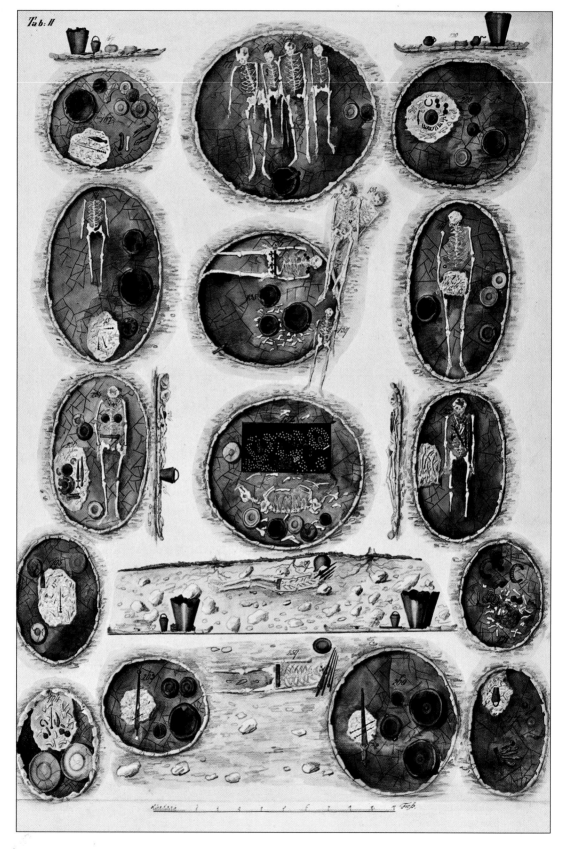

Tab: II

and fearsome warriors reached the pinnacle of their power around the third century B.C. Then their sway extended from the North Sea to the Mediterranean, and from Iberia to the Black Sea coasts, Galatia, and Anatolia. Significantly, some Celtic tribes migrated to the British Isles and Ireland, setting into motion a vital cultural evolution there.

Half a century after the Celtic tribes began their invasion of Britain, they reached Ireland. Some came by way of Britain, but others were Iberian Celts, who spoke a language somewhat different from that of the British invaders. Other tribes crossed the Alps and settled in the Po Valley, sending raiding parties through the Apennines and into Italy, culminating in the siege of Rome around 396 B.C. In 279 B.C. Celtic invaders devastated Delphi, Greece, and continued on into Asia Minor. Celtic tribes left their marks—and their names—on places throughout Europe, including Paris (the Parisii), Rheims (the Remi), Helvetia (Switzerland; the Helvetii), Belgium (the Belgae), and Bologna and Bohemia (the Boii). To the Romans, the Continental Celts were known as Galli (or Gauls), related to the Gaels in Ireland and Scotland, the Galicians in Spain and Portugal, and the Galatians in Asia Minor (to whom St. Paul sent an epistle).

None of these accomplishments was quite enough to override the Mediterranean animus toward the Celts, however. In the first century B.C., long after the Celts had sacked the Eternal City, Roman poet and philosopher Lucretius still managed to dismiss them as little more than failed farmers: "This race of men from the plains were all the harder, for hard land had borne them; built on stronger and firmer bones, and endowed with mighty sinew, they were a race undaunted by heat or cold, plague, strange new foodstuffs. For many years, among the beasts of the earth they led their life. And none was yet a driver of the curved plow, none yet could turn the soil with iron blade, nor bury a new shoot in the ground nor prune the ripened branch from the tree." Lucretius registered a tough assessment—and an incorrect one.

From their cultural pinnacle, dated at around 250 B.C., to their retreat into the hinterlands of the British Isles in the second century A.D., the Celts maintained the qualities that distinguish their noble history: intellectual and creative independence, courage and cruelty in warfare, inspiration in industrial and ornamental design, and a unique set of natural, spiritual, and cosmological beliefs. These qualities informed

Excavations of 980 Celtic tombs in Hallstatt, Austria, began in 1846. Most graves held everyday items—pots, bowls, and tools—but some contained fine bronze and gold ornaments.

successive generations and permutations of Celtic culture, from antiquity to today. Although the ultimate origins of these peoples remain shrouded in mystery, we do know that the Celtic influence—from early first-millennium migrations to later innovations in religion, myth, art, and iron-work—caused substantial social turmoil in Europe and the Mediterranean, a turmoil that lasted centuries and whose legacy enriched the world.

THE OLDEST KNOWN EVIDENCE OF THE CELTS comes from Hallstatt, Austria, near Salzburg, a large prehistoric salt-mining area where excavations have uncovered hundreds of Celtic graves dating from about 700 B.C. The Hallstatt period in European history, 750 to 450 B.C., is named for this region. The word *Hall,* frequently found in contemporary German and Austrian names for places or geographical features, is derived from an

Celtic priests often wore antler headdresses. In this silver relief from the Gundestrup Cauldron, the lord of the animals and fertility holds a ram-headed snake and a torque, or metal collar.

ancient word for salt and related to the German word *Salz.* As with other cultures during this period, salt was the primary commodity used for trading by the Celts. Valued as a meat preservative and essential for the storage of food over long winters, salt was nearly as prized as gold.

The Hallstatt Celts were among the first in northern Europe to formulate iron and to employ the strong, durable metal in weapons and tools. During the early era of Celtic culture, prosperity followed salt production. Richer mines would be discovered, as appears to have happened around 600 B.C., when a new salt mine opened at Hallein, not far from Hallstatt. A new mine opened and communities soon followed. Trade routes from Austria and central France opened up exchange with

Celtic houses in Britain and Ireland tended to be circular, like the reconstructed Pimperne

House in Hampshire, England. Celtic houses in Gaul were more often rectangular. ❈

the world south of the Alps. Rich settlements run by unified dynasties brought wealth and permanence.

The Hallstatt Celts established trade links with Mediterranean regions, for example with Massalia, a Greek colony founded in 600 B.C. in the area around present-day Marseille. Wealth depended on commercial relations with the Greeks, as exemplified in the magnificent burial of a Celtic princess at Vix, near Châtillon sur Seine, with a massive ornamented bronze punchbowl of fine Italian workmanship and other imported treasures. These early Celtic aristocrats lived in hill forts on the upper Danube and were typically buried with a complete cart to carry their possessions into the afterlife. This common practice remained unexplained, though, until 19th-century archaeological finds began to reveal the secrets of Europe's early conquerors.

Isolated in the heart of the Salzkammergut region of Austria and accessible only by river, the Hallstatt region was blessed in two ways. First, it possessed a wealth of salt mines, and second, it was remote and protected. Elements of this nascent civilization remained for centuries before archaeologists discovered them. Salt mines were noted in the 14th century, and in 1824 signs of a vast Iron Age cemetery were discovered. Beginning in 1846, excavations revealed 2,000 graves loaded with long, heavy swords, daggers, axes, cauldrons, pottery, and jewelry with striking geometric and animal motifs.

Excavation of a Celtic chieftain's tomb discovered near Hochdorf in 1978 produced landmark finds: fine gold jewelry, fragments of clothing made from richly embroidered Chinese silk, fishhooks, drinking horns, a gold drinking bowl, a bronze cauldron rimmed with lions, a large iron-trimmed wagon filled with a banquet service, and several personal items—a birch-bark hat, a wooden comb, and iron nail clippers. Iron clasps and bronze brooches gathered opulent decorative fabrics. Most strikingly, an elaborate bronze funeral bier, holding the remains of the prince (with his gold-hilted dagger), was supported by eight metal statues of women on unicycle-like wheels of bronze and iron, which enabled the bier to be rolled. Clearly the Celts sent their dead into eternity equipped to eat, drink, conquer, and rule forevermore.

THE IRON AGE OF LATE PREHISTORIC EUROPE is typically divided into two archaeological eras, the Hallstatt (750-450 B.C.) and the La Tène (450-50 B.C.). The latter, a period of spectacular achievements in ironwork, was named for a site at the east end of Switzerland's Lake Neuchâtel, where 19th-century archaeologists discovered astonishing metalwork decorated in a style that emphasized elaborate patterns of interwoven curves and spirals. The art of the La Tène Celts was an extension of the earlier Hallstatt styles, incorporating bolder and more abstract designs, and featuring highly stylized plants and animals with little resemblance to those in nature. So innovative and captivating was this nuanced decorative aesthetic that the La Tène style dominated European metalwork, enamelwork, and stone carving through the first century A.D. Its influence would last into the Middle Ages and become a fundamental element of medieval art. La Tène—style artifacts such as carved stones and bronze mirrors with bold, swirling spirals and crosshatch patterns have been excavated from several British and Irish sites dating from the late Iron Age.

For example, writes historian Barry Cunliffe in *The Extraordinary Voyage of Pytheas the Greek,* "in 1896 a farmer plowing his field at Broighter, on the shore of Lough Foyle near Limavady in County Derry, unearthed a spectacular hoard of seven gold objects that had been buried, probably in the first century B.C. or first century A.D., as an offering to the gods." The stash included "a massive gold torque with buffer terminals heavily decorated with curvilinear La Tène decoration," two other gold torques, two necklaces of gold wire, "and two gold models, one of a cauldron, the other of a boat." As Cunliffe points out, "the boat is of outstanding interest not least for the accurate structural detail that it has to offer of these early craft.... Inside were nine benches for the rowers to sit on and eighteen oars, each guided by a rowlock. At the stern was attached a large steering oar and toward the center stood a mast with a yard to take a square-rigged sail."

The archaeological evidence discovered at Hallstatt, La Tène, and other Celtic sites supports the existence of an aristocratic society with chiefs and royal families. Settlement excavations provide fascinating glimpses into the lifestyle of these early Celts. The Hallstatt and La Tène cultures can be distinguished in a number of ways. Whereas the Hallstatt elite were buried with four-wheeled wooden carts, the La Tène elders seem to have been accompanied more often by the lighter, faster two-wheeled chariots. Coinage appears to have been unknown to the Hallstatts, but the La Tène tribes produced coins of precious metals, sometimes decorating them with chariots and horses. Other coin styles were copied from the Greeks, such as one featuring the head of Apollo.

The La Tène phase is characterized by Celtic raiding and settlement in broader areas, including Britain, and the emergence, under aristocratic patronage, of Celtic art in the industrial and political heartland of the Rhineland and Upper Marne. Amphorae, or wine jars, found at burial sites attest to well-established trade routes around the Mediterranean. Growing economic strength was based on industrialization as well as trade.

Excavations uncovering such luxury items as combs and jewelry reveal that upper orders of the La Tène Celts cut quite dashing figures wherever they went. Greek historian Diodorus Siculus describes the Celtic Gauls of the first century B.C. as "tall with moist white flesh; their hair is not only naturally blond, but they also make artificial efforts to lighten its color by washing it frequently in lime water.... nobles keep their cheeks clean-shaven but let their mustaches grow long, until they cover their mouths." He called their clothes "amazing," their "tunics dyed in every color," and noted that "they pin striped cloaks on top of thick cloth in winter and light material in summer, decorated with ... multicolored squares."

Some tribes formed loose federations, but the early Celts never became a united nation. Still, at various times they controlled vast stretches of territory. Most people lived in rural settlements, raising crops and livestock, and belonged to small tribes that claimed common ancestors. There were three social levels of the tribe: The highest was the king and related aristocrats, including warriors; the second was the Druids, a learned class that included lawyers, poets, and priests recruited from warrior-class families but holding special status through education and supposed connection to the deities; the third class, the *egues*, was made up of the freemen farmers. The various Celtic tribes lacked a well-defined central government and were primarily bound together by common speech, customs, and religion.

The latter, especially, was a crucial bond in Celtic society. Each tribe had its local deities and cults, collectively forming a cosmology of hundreds of gods and goddesses. Rites were held in common because the priestly caste of Druids was a pan-Celtic institution that exercised great political influence. Druids forecast the future, educated the nobility, conserved traditions, and met annually in a solemn assembly at Chartres in Gaul, where they settled disputes between nobles and mediated tribal conflicts.

According to some reports, primarily those of Julius Caesar, the Druids also oversaw human sacrifices. "All the Gauls are keen on religious observances," he wrote. "Because of this those who contract more serious illnesses, as well as those involved in hazardous under-takings, either make or promise to make human sacrifices, and use the Druids to perform these on their behalf. The reason for this is that they believe in 'a life for a life'—otherwise the gods cannot be placated. Some of the tribes use colossal wickerwork figures, the limbs of which are filled with living men: these images are then set alight and the victims perish in a sea of flame. They think that those caught thieving or robbing or committing other crimes are particularly pleasing as sacrifices to the gods; but if they are short of such people, innocent men will serve equally well."

Of course we have no evidence that Caesar ever witnessed such scenes. His accounts of human sacrifices may well be exaggerations, even fictions, intended to demonize the Celts and paint their Druid priests as barbarians.

There is plenty of other evidence, though, to suggest that gore proved intoxicating to the Celts. In the seventh century A.D., Irish Celts were still sacrificing humans to their gods—prisoners to war gods, babies to harvest gods, explains Thomas Cahill in *How the Irish Saved Civilization*. "Believing that the human head was the seat of the soul, they displayed proudly the heads of their enemies in their temples and on their

This fine bronze flesh fork, left, was designed for piercing meat. Ornamented with water birds, it dates from the seventh or eighth century B.C. The bronze figure of a dancing girl, above, reinforces the belief that Celtic women were tall.

*Life-size limestone carving depicting Janus, the double-headed deity, guarded a pre-Roman
Celtic sanctuary north of Marseille, France, at the mouth of the Rhône River.*

palisades; they even hung them from their belts as ornaments, used them
as footballs in victory celebrations, and were fond of employing skull tops as
ceremonial drinking bowls."

Bloody human sacrifices aside, life seemed pretty good for the
Celts. They became increasingly adept at living in established, self-
sufficient tribal settlements, rearing their own livestock and trading
with countries farther afield for precious metals and other commodi-
ties. Prosperity enabled the arts to flourish and a distinctive
spirituality to emerge. But their constant desire for warfare, conquest,
and acquisition, combined with their wanderlust, pushed the Celts
into bold, sometimes foolhardy adventures.

After the third century B.C., some Celts moved into the Balkans,
including the area that is now Bulgaria and Greece. Most wars were
fought against unknown and distant societies, but disputes and fighting
did occur between the tribes themselves—a chaotic state of affairs that
stands in stark contrast to the orderly determination of the Romans, who

conquered much of Europe between about 300 B.C. and A.D. 100. Celtic tactics met with disaster in 225 B.C., when they found themselves sandwiched between two Roman armies near Telemon, Italy. Celtic warriors characteristically lacked discipline in holding formations, and this weakness led to their demise. For the next 200 years, Celts and Romans met regularly on battlefields in Europe. The same impulsive drive that enabled the Celtic migration throughout Europe made the Celts vulnerable to the steely strength of Rome's ever expanding empire.

The might of the Roman Army increased vastly during the second century B.C. First southern France, then the whole of Gaul was conquered by the Romans. Instigated by the mass migration of the Celtic Helvetii from their cramped homeland around Lake Neuchâtel to the greener pastures of the Atlantic coast of Gaul, the Romans under Caesar massacred these migrants.

"The Romans could make nothing of the Celts," historical novelist Edward Rutherfurd has determined. "A good Roman loved systematic government, hierarchy, bureaucracy: the Celts had innumerable petty chiefs and kings, tied to each other by generations of blood vows and clientships so tangled that no logical Roman could ever make sense of them. Even their gods, like the great Dagda, the protector of the tribe, seemed to take pleasure in changing into unlikely shapes and playing tricks on mankind: not to satisfy their lusts and desires—this the Romans could have understood—but for no reason at all."

One of the final battles in Gaul between the Romans and Celts ended in 52 B.C. with the defeat of Vercingetorix at Alesia ("rocky hill" in Celtic), near Alise-Sainte Reine, France, today. This young Celtic prince was Gaul's last hope. Early on he roused the countryside in revolt against the Romans, using scorched-earth tactics instead of typically haphazard Celtic raiding schemes. But he ran out of luck when not all Celts heeded his commands.

Withdrawing with 80,000 Gauls and a month of rations, Vercingetorix waited for reinforcements at Alesia. Caesar readied his 40,000 troops and fortified his position with two lines of defense encircling the weakening resistance. Six weeks into the standoff, the starving Celts fought bravely, but the Romans routed them. Vercingetorix emerged from the gates of Alesia, dressed in battle finery, and rode his horse in a ritual circle around the Roman tribunal before dismounting, relinquishing his weapons, and sitting in silent submission at Caesar's feet.

For this final act of nobility—which may have given some Celts the chance to escape with their lives—Vercingetorix was rewarded by Caesar with six years of brutal imprisonment after which he was paraded through the Roman Forum, then put to death.

No unified Celtic mythology is known, but the expansive Celtic pantheon suggests a loose association of beliefs. Like the Greeks and Romans, the Celts were highly religious and superstitious people who invoked a deity for nearly every phase of human experience. Their religion was by no means a simple affair; the supernatural pervaded every aspect of life. Spirits were everywhere and gods were ever present, controlling the natural world and commanding the seasons. They were needy deities who demanded constant attention and placation. The Druids served as inter-mediaries, since they knew the ancient wisdom and could win the favor of the divine.

William Stukeley's fanciful conception of a Druid, shown in this 1740 illustration, suggests the trappings of monastic mysticism associated with the Celtic order.

The privileged caste and order of religious scholars known as Druids—a word that may mean "knowledge of the oaks"— were essential to Celtic society. According to Caesar, the Druids' duties were to "officiate at the worship of the gods, regulate public and private sacrifices, and give rulings on all religious questions. Large numbers of young men flock to them for instruction.... They act as judges in practically all disputes whether between tribes or between individuals."

Druids administered the system of religious and secular learning and literature; they oversaw social, political, and religious affairs and events. At the height of the Celtic influence in Europe, Druids underwent a 20-year apprenticeship in law, history, magic, astronomy, medicine, and poetry, studying at one of two major training centers, one west of Paris and one off the coast of Wales.

The Druids believed that the soul was immortal and that the soul of a man who died in battle passed quickly to another body. Although Romans were generally tolerant of foreign religions, they had no patience for Celtic druidism, which in certain areas such as Wales actively

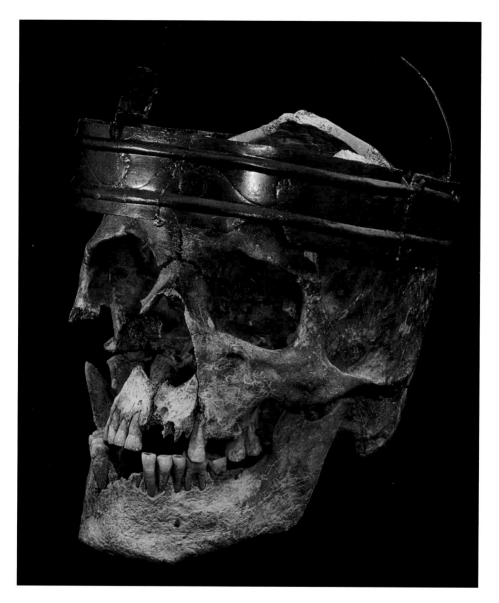

An Iron Age crown and skull came together out of a grave in Deal, England.
The headpiece may represent that its wearer enjoyed a high level of priestly authority.

resisted Roman rule. Slaughter followed, with the Romans overwhelming the Druids, outlawing their faith, and introducing a cult of emperor worship and taxation in its place. This was, not surprisingly, a detested imposition, but the ever resilient Celts worshipped their own local gods alongside the Roman imports.

No Druidic creation story survives, but the Celtic cosmology is entrenched in nature, with many accounts of the supernatural creation of islands, mountains, and forests. Divinity was perceived to reside in all

The bronze Coligny Calendar—found in Burgundy, France, and nearly 2,000 years old—records nights, not days, and lists times of good omen. The script is Roman but the words are Celtic.

corners of the natural world, particularly around springs, groves, lakes, and rivers, which frequently bore the names of their supernatural patrons. The Celts rarely enclosed their places of worship in stone temples, but instead used nature's own boundaries to define sacred space. The sun was an emblem of divine power and constancy. Many Celtic gods were female and were represented as a trinity. Most of the gods could change forms—there was no hierarchy; there were no defined roles—and many birds and animals were considered sacred. The wild boar's flesh sustained gods and heroes. The salmon taught occult wisdom. The serpent wore the horns of a ram. Many other animals provided shapes for gods to assume.

To the Romans' dismay, the Celts were lax in their religious structure and nomenclature. The conquerors simplified the cosmology by assigning Roman equivalents to tribal gods—no small task, since the Celts had more than 300 gods and goddesses. The primary pantheon, though, likely totaled about three dozen gods, including Brigid (goddess of poetry and learning), Cernunnos (lord of the animals, god of fertility), Dagda (the All-father, god of weather and crops), Danu (mother of powerful goddesses), Epona (the Divine Horse, a mother goddess), Rosmerta (goddess of abundance), and Taranis (god of thunder).

Julius Caesar's attempts to document the Celtic faith introduced more confusion than clarity. He assigned the names of Roman gods and goddesses—Mercury, Apollo, Mars, Jupiter, and Minerva among them—to Celtic deities. For example, Caesar equated the Celtic god of light, Lugh (or Lugos), to Mercury, even though they had distinctly different origins and actions. Flawed though it may be, though, Caesar's record is one of the few that exist to help assemble an understanding of the complex system of Celtic beliefs.

HALF A CENTURY BEFORE THE BIRTH OF JESUS, Romans crossed the English Channel and invaded Britain. From the second century B.C. on, Celts had established communities throughout Britain. Now they were forced again to retreat in the face of Rome's empire. "In any conflict between the Celts and Romans," writes Nora Chadwick in *The Celts*, "the superior powers of organization, sense of discipline, and general orderliness of the Roman culture were bound to overcome the volatile and undisciplined Celts whose sense of loyalty, powerful though it may have been, was normally centered on an individual rather than on an institution or an ideal."

Not all Celts submitted to Roman domination, and certainly not without a fight. Over the course of a century of campaigns, as Romans conquered Britain and Wales and made Britannia one of the 45 provinces of the Roman Empire, free-willed Celts headed to the remote corners of Cornwall, Wales, and Scotland to resist Roman occupation.

And not all resistance was carried out in the hinterlands. Boudicca, queen of the Iceni in East Anglia, took vengeance on the Romans who had flogged her and raped her daughters. She led a remarkable revolt against the Romans in A.D. 60, rampaging through Colchester, St. Albans, and even London, slaughtering subjects of the empire along the way. Roman Suetonius Paulinus retaliated, and his army eventually cut down some 80,000 Iceni. Boudicca faced total defeat; she may have taken her own life. By A.D. 78 all of Britain but northern Scotland had been brought under Roman rule. Ireland remained untouched—and profoundly Celtic.

Those Celts who didn't resist adopted many Roman traits, including the use of Latin. Celtic aristocrats moved into villas or even towns where they could manage their estates. Manufacturing increased, and a relative peace prevailed. In Northern Britain, however, the fiercely

⁂ JULIUS CAESAR ⁋

The General and the Celts

EW ACCURATE CONTEMPORARY ACCOUNTS OF THE EARLY CELTS survive, which makes the writings of Roman statesman and general Julius Caesar (100-44 B.C.) all the more valuable. In the course of his military campaigns in Europe, Caesar battled both continental Gauls and British Celts. In his *Commentaries on the Gallic War* (*Commentarii de Bello Gallico*), Caesar described Gaul's inhabitants. Although he found many of their habits barbarian, he appreciated their rustic dignity.

"The Gauls assert that they are all descended from Dis," wrote Caesar. For him, Dis was a name for Pluto, Roman god of the underworld. "This is why they reckon time by counting not days but nights; birthdays and the beginnings of months and years they regard as being the night and the following day…. They do not allow their children to associate with them openly until they are old enough for military service; it is considered disgraceful for a son to accompany his father in public whilst still a child."

"Husbands have the power of life and death over both children and wives," wrote Caesar. "Their funerals are sumptuous and magnificent. Everything that the dead man held dear while alive is thrown onto the flames, even animals; and until recently slaves and dependants who were thought to be favourites were burnt all together at the end of the proper funeral ceremonies."

"Buildings are very close together," Caesar wrote of Celtic Britain. "Tin is mined inland, iron near the coast, but only in small quantities; the bronze they use is imported. As in Gaul there is wood of every kind available, except beech and pine. The meat of hare, chicken and goose is taboo to them, though they keep them for sport or as pets…. In towns which are generally held to be well run there is a law that if anyone hears a rumour affecting the public interest he should tell a magistrate, without passing it on to anyone else … The magistrates can keep secret what they think fit, and only make public what they consider advantageous. Discussions about affairs of state are only allowed in council." Approaching the Celts as a conqueror, Caesar could still write of them admiringly.

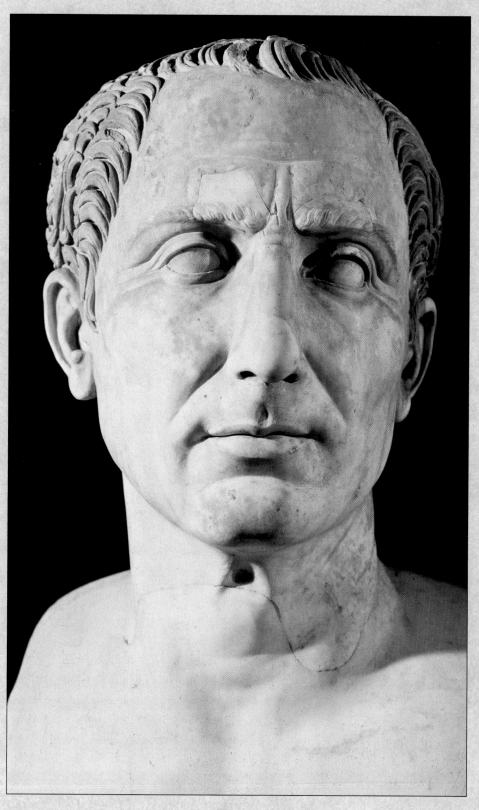

Warrior, scholar, statesman, and emperor, Julius Caesar lived from 100–44 B.C.

The stomach of Lindow Man, discovered in a bog near Manchester,
England, contained poisonous mistletoe pollen, suggesting that this
20-year-old Celt may have been sacrificed.

tribal Picts and Caledonians made imperial expansion such
an untenable goal that in 122 the Romans constructed a barrier to
partition their conquered lands from the untamable north. Hadrian's
Wall became the dividing line between Roman lands and those of the
bellicose Celts.

Cassius Dio, Roman historian of the early third century, described
the Celts as totally foreign and almost unhuman. "They dwell in tents,

naked and unshod, possess their women in common, and in common rear all the offspring," Dio wrote. "Their form of rule is democratic for the most part, and they are very fond of plundering.... For arms they have a shield and a short spear, with a bronze apple attached to the end of the spear-shaft, so that when it is shaken it may clash and terrify the enemy.... They can endure hunger and cold and any kind of hardship; for they plunge into swamps and exist there for many days with only their heads above water, and in the forests they support themselves upon bark and roots." These people, who painted pictures all over their bodies, especially horrified the Romans, who called them Picti ("painted people").

Exaggerating the animalism of the Celts, however, did not help the Romans overcome them. Vicious raids by the Emperor Severus around 208 resulted only in retrenchment. For a hundred years Hadrian's Wall succeeded in securing peace but not in enhancing Rome's empire in Britain. The people of Britain, meanwhile, adopted internationalist attitudes that came from the Roman influence of law, order, and peace. "The British thought themselves as good Romans as any," wrote Winston Churchill. "To be a citizen of Rome was to be a citizen of the world, raised upon a pedestal of unquestioned superiority over barbarians and slaves." As Britain became Anglo-Saxon and then adopted Norman feudalism, this emerging sense of cultural superiority reigned. Meanwhile Scotland remained tribally Celtic, leading to the creation of yet another distinct culture as Christianity was introduced to the British Isles and Rome's empire gradually gave way to new rulers.

In 410, Roman Emperor Honorius relinquished control of Britain and called upon the people to look toward their own defense. Saxons, Angles, and Jutes—Germanic mercenaries from Denmark and north Germany—arrived at the invitation of Vortigern, who appears to have become leader of the Britons some years after the Romans left. These Germanic tribes were to help fend off foreign incursions, but they opportunistically established their own rule. Celtic Britons fought each other and Scottish invaders as well as the Angles, the Saxons, and the Jutes. This post-Roman era has been called the Dark Ages, and the invasions, turbulence, and sweeping cultural exchange certainly made for a few unpredictable and unruly centuries.

This era was also one of accomplishment, religious development, and intellectual achievement. In the fifth century, Germanic-speaking

✖ *Human skulls—seats of the soul to the Celts—were imbedded in the*

limestone door frame of this Celto-Ligurian sanctuary near Marseille, France.

Angles created settlements that later formed the foundations of the British kingdoms of East Anglia, Mercia, and Northumbria. The Angles gave their name to their new home, which came to be called Angleland— or England. The Saxons, a Germanic tribe that had been continental neighbors of the Angles, arrived later and formed settlements that grew into the kingdoms of Sussex, Wessex, and Essex. In time the Saxons expanded their territory, pushing the Britons farther west. Britain was uncomfortably partitioned, with the Saxons in the East, the pure Celtic Irish in the West, and the Romano-British squeezed in between. The situation eased when Welsh and Cornish communities migrated to Brittany—Amorica, as it was known then—and carried their distinctive Celtic language and culture to this peninsula in northwest France.

As England was being wrested from the Romanized Celts, Celtic missionaries were effecting the spiritual conquest of Ireland. For decades Irish chieftains had preyed on Roman Britain, launching well-organized raids that won them booty and slaves. One raiding party returned to Ireland with a teenaged slave who would eventually change the country forever: Patricius Magonus Sucatus. A passionate young man, Patricius worked for six years as a herdsman before he escaped servitude and followed his spiritual calling to Gaul, then returned to Britain, where a vision seized him and he became inspired to Christianize Ireland.

Neither the Romans nor the Saxons had made it to Ireland. Some European invaders and migrants—Scandinavians and French-speaking Anglo-Normans from England and Wales—had made it to Ireland's shores, but the land Patricius encountered in 432 remained relatively undisturbed by outside influences. In those times, Ireland was a jigsaw puzzle of competing alliances. The island was divided into five provinces, or fifths: Ulster in the north, Leinster in the east, Connacht in the west, Munster in the south, and Meath, wedged in the central east coast between Ulster and Leinster.

Patricius gained his first converts at Tara, in Meath. They defied the pagan priests there by kindling an Easter fire on Slane, a hill nearby. The pagan people in the area were at first indignant, but soon they proved receptive to Patricius's gospel message, which traveled quickly through this land of half a million inhabitants. Patricius understood the social structure of the country, and he wisely observed it as he proceeded to convert the pagans tribe by tribe. As faith in the Christian message spread, kings throughout Ireland contributed land on which churches could be founded. Christianity was gradually adopted, and the old religion of the Druids either faded away or mutated into a Christianized hybrid, with ancient festivals turned into holy days and pagan gods transformed into saints.

Patricius codified the traditional laws of Ireland as well, harmonizing them with Christian practice and mitigating harsh laws about slavery and taxation of the poor. He introduced the Roman alphabet and initiated monastic strongholds that served as beacons of faith not only for Ireland but for the whole of Europe in the dark centuries to come. The monastic life suited many of those with ancient Celtic roots. A monastic community appeared to be a faithful tribe led by an abbot. Thanks to established trade routes, the Irish monastic tradition influenced the entire Christianized Mediterranean. It was an echo of the Druidic spirit that had sustained the Celtic people for centuries. Patricius died in 461. Later this Romanized Celtic Briton, a zealous missionary, became known to the world as St. Patrick, patron saint of Ireland.

The fifth-century beginnings of the Christian monastic system in Ireland also nurtured the spiritual zeal that in the coming centuries would produce illuminated gospel books, the greatest masterpieces of Celtic art. Within the monasteries, scribes copied and illuminated sacred manuscripts. Knowledge of Latin awakened interest in ancient culture, and Celtic aesthetic styles—dominated by curvilinear La Tène designs—were reborn in the new Christian iconography and served as the inspiration for much manuscript illumination and many devotional objects.

One perennial example of how Celtic artistic traditions intersected with Christian tradition is the Celtic cross, carved in stone, pagan in origin and predating Christianity by centuries, yet adopted to use in many Irish and other cathedrals. "In its early form it was devoid of decorations, and the top three arms of the cross (representing the male reproductive power) were totally enclosed within the circle (representing the female reproductive power)," writes iconographer Douglas Keister about the Celtic cross. "The symbolism of the Irish cross is strongly tied to Mother Earth and national pride. The four arms can represent the four elements: air, earth, fire, water. In some Celtic crosses the four arms correspond with four provinces of Ireland, with the circle used in creating a fifth province by incorporating pieces of the other four." The coming influence of the Christian religion evoked small changes in the shape of the indigenous cross. "As Christianity was adopted by the Celts, the circle began to get smaller," Keister describes, "symbolizing either the triumph of Christianity or the loss of the Goddess influence."

The Christian presence, especially in the monasteries, elevated the importance of writing throughout Ireland. New literary works of art were

created and ancient oral traditions and legends were transcribed. Sagas of warrior kings such as Tara's Cormac Mac Airt and Ulster's Connor Mac Nessa, of wicked queens like Maeve of Connacht, and of unforgettable heroes like Cú Chulainn of *The Cattle Raid of Cooley* were documented for the first time. The long and colorful history of pagan Ireland, with its magical world of gods and beasts, sorcery and enchantment, its queens and princes, its Druid priests and poets, passed on for centuries through a rich oral tradition, now would be preserved in writing.

As Celtic Christianity flourished in Ireland, Roman Catholicism took hold of the Continent. Only the pagan English resisted this tidal wave of religious conversion. All began to change in England, however, when a Roman Benedictine monk and librarian named Augustine—later Saint Augustine of Canterbury—was dispatched in 597 by Pope Gregory I to convert the Anglo-Saxons.

Augustine was well received by King Ethelbert, who met with him near present-day Ebbsfleet. Ethelbert converted, becoming the first Christian king in Anglo-Saxon England, and in 40 years' time most of England had turned to Christianity. Ethelbert gave Augustine and his monks land at Canterbury, where they built a church and monastery. The present-day cathedral stands on that land. Augustine's further mission was to assure that more indulgent Roman ways dominated over the austerities of the Celtic monks. This deed was eventually accomplished in 663 at the Synod of Whitby. Celtic and Christian devotees agreed on celebrating Easter, but they did not agree on how to determine on what day the holiday fell from year to year. As a result of the historic gathering in Whitby, the method for setting Easter's date was codified.

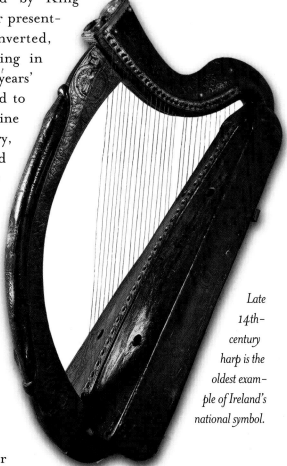

Late 14th-century harp is the oldest example of Ireland's national symbol.

Mystical animal head, opposite, adds bronze interest to a Czech wooden pitcher.

❖ Celtic Gospels ❖

The Book of Kells, the Lindisfarne Gospels, and the Book of Durrow

ORK OF AN ANGEL," ENTHUSED A VISITOR TO IRELAND IN 1185, entranced with the beauty he saw in the manuscripts of the monasteries. These illuminated manuscripts presented the four Christian gospels—Matthew, Mark, Luke, and John—in a richly ornamental Celtic style. Monks used precise drawing instruments and vivid inks on fine calfskin to create interlacing patterns, neverending spirals, and magical beasts that not only decorate but also elucidate the text. The "eternal knot" characteristic of Celtic book decoration, for example, symbolized the boundlessness of God and the infinite diversity of creation.

Medieval gospel texts reached a splendid zenith in the *Book of Kells,* a magnificent manuscript illuminated with brilliant pigments made from natural ingredients. Blue—the most precious of colors, hence sparingly used—came from powdered lapis lazuli stone obtained from Afghanistan. Glowing touches come not from gold leaf but from a yellow mineral.

The eighth-century *Lindisfarne Gospels,* another Celtic masterwork, was written and illuminated on tiny Lindisfarne (Holy Island) off the coast of Northumbria. "Eadfrith, Bishop of the Lindisfarne Church, originally wrote this book, for God and Saint Cuthbert and, jointly, for all the Saints whose relics are in the Island," wrote Aldred, a tenth-century Irish priest, on the book's last page. "And Ethelwald, Bishop of the Lindisfarne islanders, impressed it on the outside and covered it, as he well knew how to do. And Billfrith, the anchorite, forged the ornaments which are on it on the outside and adorned it with gold and with gems and with gilded-over silver, pure metal. And Aldred, unworthy and most miserable priest, glossed it in English between the lines with the help of God and Saint Cuthbert."

The earliest known Irish illuminated gospel book dates from around 670: the *Book of Durrow,* named for a monastery in County Meath founded by St. Columba. All these early manuscripts help document the dispersion of Celtic art and design from these monasteries in Ireland, western Scotland, and Northumbria to regions throughout Europe.

The traditional tools of the scribe—a quill pen and a small inkpot—were used to decorate this portrait of St. John the Evangelist in the Book of Kells. *Created in a Columban monastery (probably Iona) around* A.D. *800, these brilliantly illuminated gospels, which display delicate, intricate ornamentation, stand out as the supreme achievement of Irish Celtic art.*

The decision represents a turning point in the history of England and in the history of the Christian church. From then on, England nominally abandoned all Celtic practices. Although the west, notably Wales and West Wales (Dumnonia), retained ancient allegiances, the Celts had again been marginalized by the Romans. In the centuries to come, churches would continue to spring up across England. Pious landowners would attempt to secure favor in the afterlife by contributing land and funds to monasteries, which soon accumulated huge wealth and influence.

This period of history was to become known as the age of saints—a time when the growth of Christian monasteries cast light into the shadows of the Dark Ages. And it was Ireland that provided the illuminations, figuratively and literally, that guided Britain's conversion.

Among the religious houses founded by Celtic missionaries was the now-famous monastery established in about 563 on the Isle of Iona, just off the Pictish coast in the west of Scotland. Its founder, Columba (or Columcille), a missionary monk and warrior from Ulster, descended from royalty, had already started monasteries in Derry, Durrow, and Kells. In time this tireless clergyman would become known to the world as Saint Columba, and Iona would become a renowned center of Christian learning and missionary zeal, a monastery that for almost two centuries radiated a spiritual light through the darkness of the known world.

A few years later Columba traveled to the northern Pictish lands and converted the people and their king to Christianity. Along the way, he established missions. But it was from Iona, called a "Nursery of Saints" and the "Oracle of the West," that a golden age of art and scholarship would originate, its most magnificent expressions Celt-inspired illuminated gospels and manuscripts.

THE CELTIC CHURCH PLAYED A PIVOTAL ROLE in preserving and developing Western culture at a time when the continent of Europe was little more than an anarchic confusion of self-seeking nations. The Celts' emphasis on religion naturally put them in this position. Caesar described the Gauls as "completely addicted to religious observance," and Celtic deities persisted as objects of veneration long after their original religion had faded, honored under Roman names and later as elements in Christian ceremony. Monasteries at Clonard, Clonmacnoise, Armagh, Bangor, Lindisfarne, and Iona became great spiritual and intellectual centers.

The written word was employed to document not just religious texts but historical, legal, poetic, and mythical texts as well. "The most striking quality about the early medieval Celtic literatures, the more striking when one compares other contemporary literatures of Europe," writes historian K. H. Jackson, "is their power of vivid imagination and freshness of approach; as if every poet, gifted with a high degree of imaginative insight, rediscovered the world for himself." While literature written within other medieval cultures turned out "conventional and even hackneyed," argues Jackson, "early Celtic literature is capable of being highly original."

The Celts may never have had a unified nation, but they did share a language. They respected a good orator, and they gave poets and bards a high place in society. Asking why the Celts came to hold such a remarkable place in history, Edward Rutherfurd concludes that it must have been their genius. "Nothing showed their genius better than the extraordinary language they used, which was adopted wherever they settled and which became, by Julius Caesar's time, the lingua franca of all northern Europe," he explains. "The Celtic language was rich; it was poetic, mystical, impassioned. With this language they created their legends, their visions and their epic tales which have passed down the centuries to present times."

The language spoken by the Celts as they emerged from south-central Europe in the fifth century B.C. has been termed proto-Celtic. Soon it developed into other continental Celtic dialects. Some Celts went into the Balkans and Asia Minor; their Galatian language remained in use until the fifth century A.D. Other Celts went into Spain, where inscriptions in their Celtiberian language have been found. Celtic dialects in the British Isles divided into two branches: Brythonic and Goidelic.

Anglo-Saxon invasions in the fifth century A.D. pushed the British Celts to the northwest, creating more dialects. Brythonic Celtic in Cornwall and Devon developed into Cornish; in Wales, the ancient language evolved into Welsh; in Cumbria and parts of Scotland, it evolved into Cumbric. When Celts moved to Brittany in the fifth and sixth centuries, the Celtic derivative language in that region, Breton, began to evolve.

As Druid influences weakened and Christian influences grew, writing became widely practiced for the first time in Celtic history. Some early Celts borrowed the Greek alphabet in order to write down words from their own language, but few examples have been found. In the early Christian era, the Irish Celts used a primitive form of druidic writing called Ogham, a system of slashes and notches that allowed them to record ceremonies. Examples survive today in stone inscriptions.

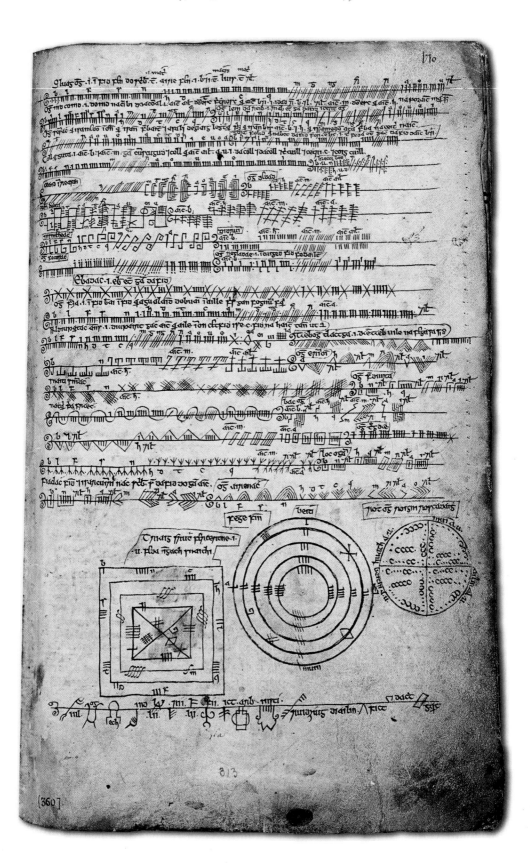

During the early Middle Ages, the Celts adopted the Roman alphabet and developed a large body of written literature including a great number of myths and legends. "As the melting pot in which Latin intelligence and Celtic inventiveness coalesced from a very early date, Ireland has preserved its ancestral traditions better than any other Western European country," writes Jean Markale in *Celtic Civilization*. "The ancient figure of Cú Chulainn composing and chanting his poems on his war chariot emerges clearer than ever as the Irish rediscover that mighty blast of destructiveness which animated the old heroes of the sagas."

National mythic epics inspired Irish lyrical poetry, and the poems—which tell of fabulous exploits, miracles, and heroes—retain an inherent sacredness. The greatest tale of the Ulster Cycle, probably the greatest tale in all early Irish literature, is *The Cattle Raid of Cooley* (*Táin Bó Cúalnge*, or simply the *Táin*), which tells the heroic exploits of Cú Chulainn, an Irish Achilles, the son of divinity who died young but died gloriously.

The earliest versions of this prose epic date from the 8th century, other versions from the 11th and 13th centuries. According to legend, Cú Chulainn was such a warrior that he would tolerate living only one day and one night, provided the tale of his accomplishments lived on forever. He could magically rouse himself into a frenzy, from which even a hundred naked women could not distract him. After killing many enemies, he fell into a trance, after which a radiance emanated from him that lasted until his spectacular death.

More than Britain, Ireland retained its mythical tradition after the rapid influx of Christianity. The Celts were an ancient people, and the new religion simply skimmed the surface of their myths. "Even within its most historical utterances, Gaelic poetry is wholly transfused by myths," Celtic historian Markale writes, pointing out the mythic core of Irish poetry. "The myth acts as a kind of corner stone for the entire poetical structure, a skeleton around which the living flesh of verse can bloom. It is myths which have given Gaelic poetry that extraordinary wealth of ideas and daring which make it so fresh and powerful. And it is his sense of the magical

Along with a guide to the ancient Ogham script, left, the 14th-century Book of Ballymote *contains Irish sagas, law texts, and genealogies. La Tène—style curves, right, decorate a mirror dating from the late first century* B.C.

The torque or metal neck ring, above, most emblematic of all Celtic jewelry, was frequently coveted among the spoils of war. The stone bust, right, adorned with a torque, was found in Bohemia and may represent a Celtic god.

which enables the poet to let his imagination run wild and free." For example, here is a description of the wondrous land of the fairies, voiced by Cú Chulainn's driver, Loeg, in *The Jealousy of Emer*:

> *The beds have posts the colour of blood*
> *and fine, gilded columns.*
> *The lamp which lights them*
> *is a radiant jewel.*

Well into the seventh century and beyond, the spirit of the Celtic imagination maintained its powerful influence. The Christian Church absorbed much of Celtic religion. Pagan gods and goddesses became Christian saints; sacred springs and wells took on new associations; cathedrals were built on many pagan temple sites. Monastic settlements such as Lindisfarne, Kells, and Iona were celebrated for their miraculous work in preserving the histories of God and man. It was the finest flowering of Celtic genius.

But this hard-won peace in the age of saints proved frightfully vulnerable to human wrath. In the last decade of the eighth century, without warning or provocation, a seaborne raid delivered an unimaginable new terror. The Vikings arrived, bringing with them a dragonlike wave of destruction, fury, and bloodshed.

❊ *Weatherbeaten stone cross on Ireland's Great Skellig, more than a thousand years old,*

may mark the grave of an early monk at this ancient monastic settlement. ✳

CHAPTER 3

THE VIKINGS
Raiders and Traders of the North Seas

A FURORE NORMANNORUM
LIBERA NOS, DOMINE.
From the fury of the Northmen
deliver us, O Lord.
—NINTH-CENTURY PRAYER
COMMONLY SPOKEN IN
FRENCH CHURCHES

Like a sea dragon, this reconstructed Viking ship skims the waters of Roskilde Fjord, near Copenhagen.

Viking-age boot found in Yorkshire, England, circa A.D. 1000

 ARELY HAS A CULTURE PRESENTED ITSELF TO THE WORLD with the blunt ferocity of the Norsemen, who raged into history on June 8, 793, with a merciless assault on the monastery at Lindisfarne (Holy Island) off the northeastern English coast. Although windswept and bare, the Holy Island was a garden of scholarship in the depths of the Dark Ages. The church and monastery, built around 635, represented the first establishment of Celtic Christianity in England. Here peaceful monks, immersed in devotions, created one of the most spectacular manuscripts in the world, the *Lindisfarne Gospels.* The monastery was a treasury holding material as well as spiritual wealth, but in eighth-century England there were few fears for the security of a pious settlement of men engaged in God's work. In this era, England was resolutely Christian but not yet a unified nation. It was frequently beset by the tireless feuding of its various kingdoms, but it was a relatively peaceful and prosperous island that believed itself secure from outside attack.

Then came the Vikings.

Wood carving from Hylestad stave church in Norway depicts the blacksmith Regin reforging the mythical hero Sigurd's sword, so he can slay the dragon Fafnir and steal his treasure.

"Never before has such terror appeared in Britain as we have now suffered from a pagan race," lamented the scholar Alcuin at the time. The Vikings "desecrated the sanctuaries of God, and poured out the blood of saints around the altar, laid waste the house of our hope, trampled on the bodies of saints in the temple of God." More succinctly, the *Anglo-Saxon Chronicle* records: "The harrying of the heathen miserably destroyed god's church in Lindisfarne by rapine and slaughter."

Both assessments understate the atrocity carried out by the ship-borne raiders from across the North Sea. They plundered Lindisfarne, slaughtered clergy or carried them off as slaves, brutalized, burned, and otherwise terrified the island. Arriving and departing on sleek boats called *drakkars* adorned with outrageous heads of serpents and dragons, the heathen Vikings soon rattled England to her bones. And the horror that descended upon Lindisfarne—the best documented, though not the first Viking raid— soon swept the English, Irish, Scottish, and Gaulish monasteries of Jarrow, Iona, Morganwg, Monkwearmouth, and Rechru on Lambey Island, too.

The Vikings ransacked the settlement of Iona in 795 and razed its early monastery. The monks rebuilt, but Vikings returned in 802 and 806. As the great monastic treasuries fell to the Vikings, precious books and metalware were buried or sent inland for security. Early in the ninth century the *Book of Kells* was sequestered inland, but even this was not enough protection. The treasured manuscript was stolen and, "after twenty nights and two months," rediscovered, "its gold having been stolen off it, and a sod [placed] over it." With each raid lives were lost, sacred ornaments looted, libraries burned.

For nearly 300 years there would be little relief from this Nordic fury. Daylight raids *(strandhögg)* carried out in the summers of the late eighth and early ninth centuries victimized the clergy, who were ideally situated to spread the word, and sometimes exaggerate, the barbarianism of these Nordic invaders. "The Vikings' victims gave them such bad press that they have never lived it down," writes political historian Tony Griffiths. "Despite the efforts of some scholars, who have pointed out the constructive aspects of Viking settlement, illustrated by recent archaeological digs..., the Vikings have kept the reputation acquired from Irish churchmen and French poets who witnessed their destructive energy."

Viking raids targeted small, poorly defended towns and isolated farms. Their primary bounty was cattle, horses, and food. Churches and monasteries were early favorite targets because they were largely defenseless and contained untold treasure, such as beautiful ivory croziers and books covered with gold and precious stones. The Vikings became known for

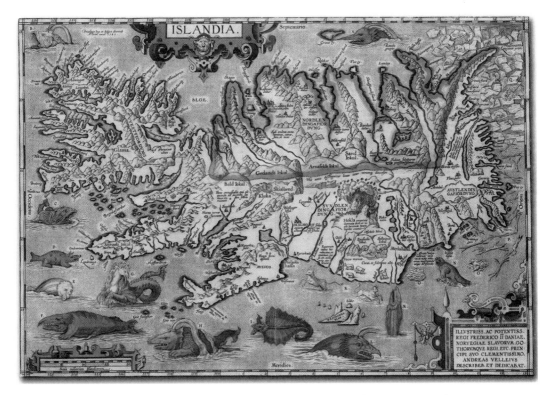

Snarling sea monsters protect Iceland's fjords and uplands in this 16th-century Dutch engraving.

surprise attacks and quick retreats. They could row their light, swift ships into shallow rivers and drag them ashore easily. To place Viking rage in historical context, however, it should be noted that extreme violence was a common response to many a problem throughout Europe in this age. The Christian leader Charlemagne had executed 4,500 Saxons at Verden in 782, years before the Vikings directed their first Dorset coast assault.

Over the span of a quarter millennium—from an initial raid on Wessex in the 790s into the 11th century—Viking civilization dominated Europe. Its domain faded first in 1042 with the end of Danish rule of England, and finally in 1066 with the Norman conquest of England at the Battle of Hastings. But this narrow focus obscures the achievements of the Viking culture, which linked the three Scandinavian proto-nations: Denmark, Norway, and Sweden.

These lands were held together by kings, but their boundaries were for-ever fluctuating as powerful *jarls* (earls) within them fought for wealth and power. Each Scandinavian kingdom made its own adventurous sweeps across the known and unknown world, sending traders, settlers, and raiders west to America, south to Italy, and east to Russia. The Danes circled the British Isles and coastlines of Europe. The Swedes explored Russian rivers and

crossed the Black Sea, reaching Constantinople and the Orient. The Norwegians settled Iceland and Greenland and reached North America. This surge of exploration, commerce, and colonization dwindled in the 11th century, but by then the Viking age had made its indelible mark on history.

ALTHOUGH TRACES OF HUMAN HABITATION have been found in central Jutland, or Denmark, that date back to 50,000 B.C., most of the land was still covered by ice. The first known Scandinavians, dating from around 11,000 B.C., were nomadic hunters who followed migrating reindeer. Human habitation in Norway dates to the end of the last Ice Age, around 10,000 B.C., when the retreating ice carved narrow inlets, or fjords. Melting glaciers changed the shape of the land; warmer temperatures encouraged forests. Nomadic and seminomadic cultures flourished around 6000 B.C. At about the same time, ancient Scandinavians first began plying the seas in primitive boats, light ashwood canoes treated with oil or whale blubber and lashed together with leather.

Stone Age farmers had developed agricultural methods by the fourth millennium B.C. By the Iron Age, some time after 3000 B.C., they lived in permanent villages. By about 2000 B.C., Germanic peoples began a northward migration from the region of northwestern Europe by the Rhine, Danube, and Vistula Rivers. These were the future Vikings. They moved into a Scandinavian homeland with fjords, rivers, inlets, and open ocean but limited arable soil and timber. The landscape quickly inspired skills in boat craftsmanship and ocean navigation.

After 2000 B.C. and the coming of the Bronze Age, tools improved. Gold and bronze jewelry was produced in abundance, and wool was woven into garment textiles. Large archaeological finds of ornaments and weaponry from this period suggest skilled craftsmen and elaborate rites and beliefs. Autonomous Norse-speaking tribes developed trade routes, and some acquired fur, amber, copper, and tin. Such progress continued into the last centuries B.C., when a Celtic advance westward across Europe interrupted the flourishing trade of the Swedish settlers with the Mediterranean world and isolated Scandinavia from the early Iron Age. Permanent settlement and communal farming took hold, providing winter shelter and storage. Battles for territorial control saw the emergence of a ruling warrior class in the Scandinavian protonations.

Inscribed within the snake figure on this 11th–century Viking stone are runes in honor of a young Swede who died far from home. Snakes were potent symbols in Norse mythology.

Expansion of the Roman Empire in the first and second centuries A.D. revived Mediterranean trading links. A new knowledge of iron improved agriculture but increased piracy and military prowess. Nordic kingdoms dominated their Baltic neighbors, taking tribute in the form of amber, wax, fish, ivory, and furs. By the middle of the eighth century, Norway had become a country of small, independent kingships. Denmark, settled around A.D. 500 by a tribe from Sweden, united under King Godfred. The Svear tribe formed the nucleus of an emergent kingdom. *Svear rike* means the kingdom of the Svear, from which derives Sverige, Sweden's modern name. Lines were drawn, cultures defined, spears sharpened, and all three areas were primed for foreign adventure.

At the close of the eighth century, Scandinavia's ocean-going warriors took the British Isles by storm, sending tremors across well-established societies that were accustomed to war but not to such terrifying tactics.

*These chessmen, carved from walrus ivory, were
discovered in 1851 in a hoard of 93 pieces found on the
Isle of Lewis in Scotland's Outer Hebrides, once part of the kingdom of Norway.*

Attack fleets of longships fell upon the Hebrides, Orkney, the Scottish mainland, England, and western Ireland. Local populations could offer little resistance, and the territories overrun by Vikings formed the foundation of a new Norse kingdom and a base for further attacks. Within a few decades, entire kingdoms were threatened.

The enormous success Vikings achieved as warriors is not easily explained. It is true that Europe's stable states were continually battling each other, and the Vikings "came at a point when firm government, in the hands of rulers like Offa (died 796) in the English kingdom of

ABOVE: *A stone carving depicts the Viking sacking in A.D. 793 of the Holy Island, or Lindisfarne, a small, vulnerable island off England's Northumberland coast, and a symbol of the Christian Church in Anglo-Saxon England.*

RIGHT: *Ruins tell the tale of time's ravages on Lindisfarne. The monastery established here in A.D. 635 gained fame for its brilliant gospels. It was repeatedly raided by Vikings from the eighth century on.*

Mercia, and Charlemagne (circa 742-814) on the Continent, had been restoring order after the troubled centuries following the collapse of the Roman Empire," explains historian Tony Allan. Amid the renewed order, says Allan, "the pagan Vikings seemed embodiments of terror and destruction, sent by a righteous God to punish a wicked world."

Population growth, clan discord, and climate change in Scandinavia may have helped launch the Viking age. Historians have speculated that overpopulation and food scarcity provided one incentive for Vikings to move beyond Nordic lands—although modern anthropological studies of Norse skeletons indicate that a protein-rich diet enabled Vikings to grow inches taller and likely much stronger than their European neighbors. The raiding age may also have started once Norsemen developed new technologies of metallurgy. With iron enough to forge weapons and arm everyone setting off on raids, Vikings could gain the upper hand.

More than any other technology, though, it was the Viking longship that made expansion possible. The lithe, swift Norse vessels were designed for rocky fjords and storm-tossed seas. Narrow oak hulls could take a heavy load and, with their shallow draft, could land onshore. They could be rowed in calm waters or equipped with sails to catch the wind. Some boats could carry a crew of 200 men or more.

Viking shipbuilders strove to construct lightweight, flexible vessels, pliant to the forces of sea and wind, thereby working with the elements instead of against them. The ships' hulls and finely curved bows were built on a solid keel, which formed the backbone of the vessel. Boat construction employed a distinctly northern European technique called lapstrake, in which each hull plank overlaps its neighbor. Strakes were attached to keel and stem and bolted to each other with iron rivets, then ribs made from naturally curved trees were bound to the strakes as well. Cross supports at the water line supplied lateral support. Stout, solid logs braced the mast. Square-rigged sails flew from a midship mast. Elaborate carvings and bronze weathervanes adorned the prow and stern with writhing mythological beasts.

"Viking poets waxed lyrical about their ships," writes archaeologist Magnus Magnusson. "The ship was an 'oar-steed,' a 'horse of the break-ers,' an 'ocean-striding bison,' a 'surf-dragon,' a 'fjord-elk,' a 'horse of the lobster's heath'; a flotilla of ships was a 'fleet of the otter's world.' To the Viking, his ship was not just his means of transport; it was his home, his way of life, his pilgrim's way, something to love but also to fear." He quotes from an Anglo-Saxon poem, "The Seafarer":

> Bitter cares have I often harboured,
> And often learned how troubled a home
> Is a ship in a storm, when I took my turn
> At the arduous night-watch at the vessel's prow
> As it beat past cliffs. . . .
> Yet now once more
> My heart's blood stirs me to try again
> The towering seas, the salt waves' play;
> My heart's desires always urge me
> To go on the journey, to visit the lands
> Of foreign peoples far over sea...

Ships held great symbolic significance. Viking graves dating from between A.D. 400 and 1000 fill a field in Lindholm, Denmark. Those from 800 on are often topped with ship-shaped monuments. The rich were interred in boats, and the less wealthy were placed in tombs marked by rocks in ships' outlines. Most of the bodies were cremated, but the graves portray the belief that the souls of the deceased were embarking on a journey. The Vikings believed that dead warriors went to Valhalla, the "hall of heroes," where they ate, drank, and kept in fighting form. Weapons were typically buried alongside warriors: double-edged longswords, wooden shields with iron centerpieces, battle axes, and richly decorated spears.

A dead warrior reached Valhalla more quickly by being burned in his ship, belongings by his side. For the burial, a ship was drawn up on land and placed into a pit. A burial chamber was constructed behind the mast, where the deceased, dressed in finery, was placed on a bed. Copious provisions were provided, dogs and horses sometimes sacrificed. Atop the vessel, a funeral pyre was built. The ship and its contents were set aflame, then a burial mound was constructed over the ashes.

An account of a spectacular Viking cremation was left to us by the Arab chronicler Ibn Fadlan, who happened upon a group of Rus Vikings burying a chieftain on the banks of the Volga in 992. "They gather his wealth and divide it in three—one part for his family, one part to provide clothes for him, and a third part for *nabidh* [a fermented drink]." A horse, cows, a hunting dog, and a slave woman were all sacrificed for the burial. Aboard the ship, writes Ibn Fadlan, waited an old woman called the Angel of Death, assigned to kill the slave. "Lo, I see my lord and master," the sacrificial slave said. "He calls to me." She drank from a cup of nabidh and sang a long song—so long, in fact, that the old woman told her to hurry up! Finally the girl entered the burial tent, and the Angel of Death stabbed and strangled her, then placed her body beside her master's. "Each man carried a firebrand," Fadlan describes, "which he threw upon the woodpile, so that the wood was engulfed in flames, then the ship, the tent and the man, the slave and everything."

THE NAME "VIKING" probably comes from the Old Norse word *vik*, meaning "bay" or "creek," but some ancient sources record the word as a verb rather than a noun; to go "a-viking" meant to embark on an expedition of piracy and plunder. Then, adopted by the Scandinavians in the ninth century, the word meant a sea voyage.

Viking leaders were likely warlords who had been displaced by more powerful kings. At this time in Scandinavia, society was strictly divided into classes. The lowest class was the thralls, or slaves, who labored on the farms. As raids progressed, the thrall class became populated by non-Nordic people captured in Western Europe. The middle class was composed of the *karls,* free peasants and merchants who either owned land or worked the land of a jarl, or aristocrat. Nobility included the kings, chiefs, and other people with great wealth or highly honored ancestors. The karls were the most apt to go marauding, since wealth and land were the only ways out of the class, but few Scandinavians spent all their time going a-viking. Most worked as farmers or merchants and participated in seasonal raids on wealthy towns, monasteries, and churches.

Seasonal though they may have been, those raids were spectacular and unprecedented. Sleek ships enabled the Vikings to travel farther than ever before. The 200 years that followed the hit-and-run devastations on Wessex and Lindisfarne are almost defined by the Viking menace. Ships "attacked all the coasts of Europe," writes historian Arne Emil

Odin is the chief Viking god, a fearless fighter and brilliant poet. He gave one of his eyes to the giant Mimir, guardian of the Well of Wisdom, for knowledge of the past, present, and future.

Christensen. "Vikings sailed up the rivers of France and Spain, conquered most of Ireland and large sections of England, and assumed control of areas skirting rivers in Russia and the Baltic coast. These are narratives of raids in the Mediterranean, and as far east as the Caspian Sea. Norsemen starting out from Kiev were even foolhardy enough to attempt an attack on Constantinople, the capital of the Byzantine Empire."

Over time, colonization replaced these plundering raids. Place-names reveal a large Viking population in northern England near York. Farther south in Britain, a large area was called the Danelaw, so named because Danish laws and customs prevailed there. Alfred, King of Wessex, brokered an uneasy peace with the Danes, thus ensuring the existence of Wessex and Mercia and, by extension, England. The Frankish King Charles III gave Normandy as a fief to Rollo, a Viking chieftain. The islands north of Scotland developed a mixed Celtic-Norse population, and Viking societies thrived on Iceland and Greenland. Around A.D. 1000, people from Iceland or Greenland discovered land to the west, and the sagas tell of several journeys including attempts to plant roots in the new land later named North America.

In 991 a large party of Scandinavian raiders met English defense forces on the estuary of the Blackwater River (the Pant), near Maldon in Essex, where Vikings had already raided a number of seaports. This Viking raid inspired *The Battle of Maldon,* the last of the Old English heroic narratives:

> The slaughter-wolves advanced, minded not the water, a host of Vikings westward over the Pant, over the bright water bore their shields... Now was combat near, glory in battle. The time had come when doomed men should fall. Shouts were raised; ravens circled, the eagle eager for food. On earth there was uproar. They let the file-hard spears fly from their hands, grim-ground javelins. Bows were busy, shield felt point. Bitter was the battle-rush. On either side warriors fell, young men lay dead.

In early Viking raids, small, fast-moving forces attacked by sea, targeting monastic settlements on islands and coasts. They disappeared with equal rapidity. Later, Vikings became capable of mounting large-scale assaults. In 885-886, 40,000 Danish Vikings poured out of 700 longships and laid siege to Paris for 11 months. They were finally paid 700 pounds of silver by King Charles the Fat, who sent them to Burgundy. In 994 a force of 95 ships entered the Thames to block and assault London, only to be driven back by the city's army. In 1013 the Danes launched a full-force invasion upon London. They drove out King Ethelred and captured the city, but Ethelred returned with Olaf of Norway and took it back. At the same time the rest of the British Isles were preoccupied with the struggle between Vikings and the Celtic Irish. Frequently the Celts attacked and slaughtered Viking parties. Celts held fast the interior of Ireland against fortified Viking settlements on the coast, finally meeting those Norsemen at Clontarf in 1014.

Viking patterns of attack and settlement were dictated by the geography of the Scandinavian countries. In the east, Swedes headed across the Baltic, navigating the Volga and Dnieper Rivers and founding Novogrodka and Kiev

⫸ *Iceland's Axe River flows through the massive lava rock formations of Thingvellir,*

site of one of the world's first parliaments, which convened in A.D. 930. ✳

along the way. Russian names today such as Oleg, Igor, and Vladimir derived from the Swedish Helgi, Ingvar, and Valdemar. The Rus soon controlled a state that reached almost to the Black Sea, and even dared to attack Constantinople, the era's mightiest city. Byzantine rulers were so impressed by the bravery of these Vikings that after they had dispatched them in battle, they recruited Northmen into an elite military unit that survived for centuries. The famous Varangian Guard ("Varangian" likely deriving from *var,* meaning pledge in Old Norse) protected the emperor at home and served as imperial attack troops in the field. Even today, at the Hagia Sophia in Istanbul, you can see scratched twig-shaped runes, or Norse script, etched into a polished balustrade. By 900 the Rus had set up trade patterns with the Byzantine Empire and had staged raids across the Caspian Sea into northeast Iran. When the flow of Middle Eastern silver abated, these Scandinavians moved westward to go a-viking in England.

Danes barreled south and southwest, Norwegians sailed to the coasts of northern Europe, and these Vikings plundered every wealthy island, inlet, and stream from the North Sea to Spain in search of precious goods and metals. By about 1033 the Danes controlled England from north Yorkshire to the Thames, held sway in Normandy, and dominated trade in the Baltic. The Danelaw, a huge domain subject to Viking law, was partially unified by the official language of Norse. The Norwegians founded Dublin in 841 and then headed east to northern Britain. They settled the Faroe Islands and Iceland and even raided as far south as Moorish Spain, attacking Seville in 844. Viking fleets battered London Bridge, besieged Paris, burned Andalusian mosques, and took slaves in North Africa. They navigated the Mediterranean, looted Pisa, sailed up the Rhône to raid Arles, and may even have reached Alexandria, Egypt.

Raiders became settlers, intermingling with local populations, and the speed of Viking assimilation is noteworthy. In Dublin, for example, the Norse lost their Viking identity through intermarriage, conversion to Christianity, and adoption of the Gaelic language by the late 10th century. William the Conqueror (1028–1087) was a Norman baron, but he was also a descendent of Rollo, the Viking warrior whose army had moved into Normandy just one century before.

Viking successes indicate that some of their leaders were skillful organizers. Spheres of interest developed between Danish, Swedish, and Norwegian Vikings, and groups from all three nations often participated together on important raids when the most renowned chieftains set sail. An effective military tactic could win a battle, but the Vikings had much grander visions. They built large merchant towns in Birka, Sweden; Kaupang, Norway; and Hedeby, in what is now Germany. Excavations of these sites confirm the vital mercantile role of the Norse. The Viking kingdom in Kiev formed the basis of the Russian empire, and eventually the Vikings were to be the first Europeans to make permanent settlements on Iceland or to pass winters in Greenland, Labrador, and Newfoundland. The Norwegian anthropologist Vilhemmer Stefansson wrote in 1930 that the Viking expansion was perhaps "the only large-scale migration in history where the nobility moved out and the peasantry stayed home." Some settlements did not survive the Viking period, such as the kingdoms based in Dublin and York, but Iceland is still a thriving nation.

Of gilded bronze, this 11th-century weather-vane adorned the bow of a Viking ship and helped maintain the correct angle of the sail to the wind.

The story of the settlement of Iceland is fascinating. Around 860, setting out from Denmark's Faroe Islands, Floki of Rogaland sighted and named Iceland. Although the island was pocked by volcanoes and frosted by glaciers, there were also abundant plains and valleys, ideal for farming and raising sheep. The bays teemed with fish and birch trees abounded. In only 60 years the population jumped from zero to 70,000. When waves of Viking settlers began to arrive from Norway to Iceland in about 870, they are said to have found the books, bells, and croziers that the Papars, Irish hermit monks, had left behind as they fled the pagan seafarers. Scant archaeological evidence of pre-Viking settlement on Iceland remains, but large, hide-covered versions of Ireland's oar-propelled curraghs could have ferried the Papars to Iceland. It must have frustrated the ruddy Viking seafarers to discover that Celtic monks had beat them to Iceland.

Iceland—this partially forested, newly discovered island—offered a paradise to the Viking settlers. They organized themselves into small communities, each under a single chieftain. A great influx of new settlers from 930 onward made it necessary to divide the island into four federal parts, all governed by a general assembly called the Althing, one of the world's first parliaments.

Chiefs met annually at the rocky breach of Thingvellir, a dramatic rent in the land where the Eurasian and North American tectonic plates are forever pulling apart. At this momentous site, they convened to settle disputes among their people. "Icelanders have no other king than the laws," wrote an 11th-century German cleric. Decisions made by the Althing represented the force of the law. Clan warfare and dwindling resources ultimately impelled settlers to land farther afield, farther west.

Toward the end of the tenth century, the Viking chief Erik the Red was forced from his native Norway to Iceland "because of some killings," and in 982 he was banished from Iceland for the same reason. He sailed west to Greenland, where he found some treacherous coasts and a few welcoming fjords. Soon he persuaded several hundred Icelanders to join him in the land he called "Greenland"—something of a misnomer, since the mostly barren island was decidedly un-green—and 25 ships set sail from Iceland, carrying settlers and livestock. Tragically, only 14 of these vessels arrived. The remaining 11 ships either turned back or perished among the ice floes and northern storms.

The promised verdant land never quite materialized. Greenland lies almost entirely within the Arctic Circle, and only one-fifth of its land lies free of ice. But one promising outcome did result from the Icelanders' efforts to settle Greenland: the sighting of the continent of North America.

BJARNI HERJOLFSSON, A VIKING SEA CAPTAIN blown off his course, spotted a flat shoreline covered with woods far to the west. Although he did not pause to explore, he told the Greenland settlers about the terrain he had passed. News of this fresh source of timber was eventually bound to lure the settlers, and in about 992 Erik the Red's son, Leif the Lucky, bought Bjarni's boat and retraced his two-week, 1,800-mile voyage. Leif led the first Europeans to set foot on the new land.

Leif made three North American landings: the first in a grim, treeless placed believed to be southern Baffin Island; the second in southern Labrador, south of the medieval tree line to Markland (Wood Land), the flat, forested coast south of today's Nain; and finally the third, a place where he beached and spent a winter. It was a grassy place brimming with grapes, wheat, timber, and salmon, and he called it Vinland.

Two sagas tell the story of this adventure—*The Saga of Erik the Red* and *The Saga of the Greenlanders*. Both interpret the name "Vinland" as "wine land," saying that wine is a treasure sought by heroes. These suggestions have led to speculation that Leif's Vinland was located in what is now Maine or Massachusetts, but many historians believe Vinland was on the island of Newfoundland, noting that *vin* is Old Norse for "pasture" and suggesting that wild cranberries and lyme grass might be the vines in question. Leif's brother, Thorvald, continued the explorations, becoming the first European to encounter North American peoples, tribesmen he called Skraelings (for "screechers" or "uglies"). Apparently the natives didn't appreciate the name, because they shot Thorvald dead with an arrow.

The Norse mounted at least one major effort to colonize Vinland when Thorfinn Karlsefni—who had married Thorvald's widow, Gudrid Thorbjarnardottir—loaded three ships with 65 people and ample livestock and sailed to Leif's old winter quarters. Thorfinn's colony prospered for two years, during which time Gudrid gave birth to a boy named Snorri, the first European child born in North America. Trouble with the Skraelings forced these settlers back to Greenland after their third winter, but not before Thorfinn explored a bit. He landed at the New World Straumfjord ("steam fjord"), where Snorri was born, and Hop ("lagoon"). Scholars have variously located Straumfjord in Buzzard's Bay, Massachusetts; Long Island Sound; the Bay of Fundy; and L'Anse aux Meadows on the northern tip of Newfoundland. Hop may have been near Boston or New York City.

Of all the spots where Vikings may have landed in North America, L'Anse aux Meadows looms largest in history. This site, discovered in 1960 by Helge Ingstad and Anne Stine, preserves the most important evidence of the Vikings' presence in North America. Among all the finds, eight turf houses, enough to protect one hundred people; boat houses; hearths and cooking pots; and a bronze Viking pin match others found in Greenland and Iceland and echo information in the sagas. L'Anse aux Meadows—meadow bay—was Leif Eriksson's Vinland, or at least the gateway to it.

⊹ SHIP SHAPE ⊹

The Viking Longship

THE BASIS OF VIKING POWER WAS THE *LANGSKIP*, OR LONGSHIP, which skimmed through the frigid north seas, prow rearing over the frothy waves like a hissing sea dragon. These highly maneuverable ships were fitted with both rows of oars and a strong square sail, perpendicularly striped and made of heavy woven wool. An oak keel, sculpted for efficient turning, steadied the vessel in rough seas. The sides of the boat had vertical ribs and horizontal strakes that gave slightly when hard seas struck. A large oar on the right served as a rudder and could be lifted, allowing the boat to sail right up on a beach. Its name, *styrbord,* survives as today's term "starboard," referring to the right side of the boat. A Viking sail was about 30 feet wide. A Viking mast was short, able to be lowered into the boat for maneuverability—or for the low profile needed to make a sneak attack.

For raids to be successful, the element of surprise was essential. The tactic was to advance a swift onslaught from the sea, then beat a quick retreat before a counteroffensive could be launched. A simple raid could be carried out with just a few ships, but full-scale invasions may have involved hundreds of ships dispatching ten thousand men or more.

Life aboard was tough on these small ships. Viking sailors ate dried and salted meat and any fish caught en route. They drank sour milk, water, beer, or mead. To prevent scurvy they ate cloudberry and Scottish scurvy grass (*Cochlearia officinalis*). Each man had a chest for personal belongings, which doubled as a bench when he rowed. The first mate's back faced the port side, or *babord*. Small platforms, *lyftingar*, were mounted stern and stem.

Vikings had no magnetic compass, so navigation was conducted largely by the stars and the sun—even on overcast days. The sun stone—a mineral found in Iceland and Norway which could polarize sunlight—made it possible for sailors to locate the sun even through thick clouds or haze. Frequently birds were set free, then followed to the nearest shore.

By the late 900s Vikings had developed a system that enabled them to determine their sailing latitude. Recognizing that the sun's declination is constant at any given time of year, so long as the observer follows a straight east-west line, Nordic navigators made a table of figures that showed the sun's midday height for each week of the year. By using this table and a rudimentary gnomon—a small vertical staff in the center of a wooden disk marked with concentric circles, something like a portable sundial—a navigator could make a sighting and estimate the latitude of his ship's location. Vikings usually sailed the coastlines, but as attested by their remarkable journeys to Iceland, Greenland, and North America, they were hardly afraid to make long voyages over the open sea when the opportunity presented itself.

Vikings prepare ships for the Norman Conquest in this panel from England's Bayeux Tapestry.

Why didn't the Vikings stay in North America longer than a few decades? To be sure, they were not warmly received by the natives. Unlike the Spanish and Portuguese, who much later brought gunpowder—and germs—to the New World, the Vikings had no significant arms or population advantage. They fought Native American bows and arrows with their Viking spears and battle axes. Perhaps they attempted to stay, but there were just too few Vikings to sustain a settlement.

Contemporary scholars have a new idea: Climate change may have driven the Norse back to Scandinavia from the New World. "The great sailing trips of Leif and Thorfinn took place in the first half of the 11th century, during a climatic period in the North Atlantic called the Medieval Warming, a time of long, warm summers and scarce sea ice," writes environmental journalist Eugene Linden. "Beginning in the 12th century, however, the weather started to deteriorate with the first frissons of what scholars call the Little Ice Age, [which] probably curtailed further Norse traffic to North America."

ABOVE: *Keys dangling from a woman's belt indicated she was mistress of the farm. When Viking men were away, women managed the farm, finances, and household valuables.*

LEFT: *Icelanders replaced a Viking farmhouse destroyed by a volcanic eruption around 1104 with this reconstruction. Multiple living and work spaces include a loom room and a dairy.*

As the Viking raids tapered off around the year A.D. 1000 and trade relations established in the Viking period continued to mature, the Nordic countries emerged as a part of Christian Europe. The Vikings themselves became Christian, a conversion that had a restrictive effect on their ability to justify plunder, murder, rape, wanton destruction, and other activities that for centuries had characterized their society. Denmark, Sweden, and Norway became separate kingdoms, generally united under single monarchs, and wars were steered by the shifting alliances of the kings. Iceland had been permanently colonized, though volcanic eruptions, food shortages, and epidemics made it a perilous place to live, and Greenland persisted as a small colony for about 200 years after the last exploratory journey to North America. From 1200 to 1400, the Greenland ice cap crept toward the coast, smothering green valleys. Pack ice suffocated the fjords. As the second millennium began, all lightning raids had ended, and the era of Viking colonization was on the wane.

THREE SOURCES OF
information illuminate the Viking age and its
history. Archaeological finds reveal the tools, loot, and
material objects typical of daily life in this era. Historical records, such as
runes carved in wood and stone and written commentary left by those who
encountered the Vikings at home and abroad reveal aspects of their appearance and manner. Some documents come from clergy subjected to lightning raids, others from merchants who encountered Vikings on well-worn
trade routes. In addition to the West European narratives, writing from
other Viking contemporaries, from traveling Arabs such as Ibn Fadlan and
from the chroniclers of Byzantium, contribute to the record. And, most
wonderfully, Viking sagas themselves provide sweeping histories of entire
nations, important families, and individual northern heroes. These elaborate, creative, embellished tales—for the most part composed in Iceland in
the 13th century, some two to three centuries after the events they portray—
provide the most illuminating record of life in Viking times. By focusing
attention on actual social behaviors of people in a historical and geographical context, with a degree of attention given to fantasy, psychology, and
romance, sagas are essentially the historical novels of their time.

More than just campfire tales or family histories, the sagas explained
the very nature and purpose of Viking culture—and left us with one of the

most important examples, if not the first appearance, of the long-form narrative. Unlike the Greeks and Romans, the Vikings didn't record their tales of adventure, the events that shaped their ascendancy, or their pagan religious beliefs. In fact, they used neither pen and ink nor any kind of parchment to preserve such memories. Their runic alphabet consisted of 24 symbols, but their written records are few. Instead, the Viking oral tradition became their vibrant, brilliant art form of storytelling. Bards retold Norse poems (eddas) and epic narratives (sagas), keeping these fantastic tales alive long enough that they could eventually be transcribed by Icelandic monks in the 13th century.

The sagas are the records of Icelandic family histories. They are filled with tales of exploration, adventure, greed, feuds, jealousies, justice, and even romance. Because they were written several centuries after the events they described, their accuracy has been debated among scholars for years.

Although the stories were embellished by their authors, the sagas were, scholars believe, based on actual events. This hypothesis proved true when, in 1960, passages from *The Saga of Erik the Red* and *The Saga of the Greenlanders* (time of action: 970-1030, time of writing: 1220-1280) were used to locate the one authenticated Norse presence in North America—the remains of the Viking camp at L'Anse aux Meadows, Newfoundland.

The sagas and eddas are beyond any doubt Iceland's most important contribution to world literature. Long poems collectively called the Poetic Edda explain how the universe was formed and how humans came to inhabit the Earth. They also contain a key to understanding the myths and

Grotesque heads decorate an elaborately carved wooden sled, opposite. Above, Danish gold brooches of exceptional splendor were used by men and women to fasten cloaks.

A painted page from about 1100 shows rows of armored warriors

standing poised to plunder Angers, France, in the ninth century.

poetic language in which they were scribed—a language still legible to Icelanders today.

The Vikings spoke Old Norse, a Germanic language that had two major dialects and used an alphabet made up of characters called runes. The runic alphabet, or the *futhark* (named after its first six letters), has been preserved in about 5,000 inscriptions dating from the second century. No one knows how it originated, but it appears to have strong links to the Roman alphabet. Runes may have evolved through trade and its accompanying linguistic exchanges conducted between Roman and Germanic peoples in the Rhine area during the first century.

Runic inscriptions can be read, but their meaning is frequently cryptic, since knowledge of early Germanic languages is fuzzy as well— hence the expression "to read the runes," meaning to make an educated guess based on ambiguous evidence. Viking myth holds that the Norse god Odin first acquired the mastery of writing, and even at the time of their use, runes were considered to be esoteric signs that retained traces of primeval magic. The simplicity of these straight-line characters some-times complicates their interpretation as well. By 1066, the time of the Norman Conquest, Roman script had nearly replaced runes.

As THE VIKING PERIOD PROGRESSED, society changed and chieftains' families accumulated land and power, forming the basis for kingdoms. The Vikings' brand of paganism, with its wayward, unscrupulous deities, under-pinned their inclination to vendettas and clan warfare. Institutions slowly developed to regulate the bloodshed. Western Norway, for example, adopted the Germanic wergeld system of cash-for-injury compensation, and every free man was entitled to attend a local *thing,* or parliament. Such a council, made up of the community's nobles and freemen, made laws, decided whether the community would go to war, and held trials to judge criminals. Its decisions were more important than rulings of the king or chief. A regional *lagthing* settled larger disputes.

The Vikings were a self-sustaining agricultural society. They raised wheat, barley, oats, rye, a variety of fruits and vegetables, cattle, goats, pigs, and sheep. They supplemented their farming products by hunting deer, elk, seals, whales,

Bumpers of mead, left, were promised in Valhalla for heroes after death. Dragons, right—with scales impenetrable to swords and breath that could incinerate a shield in a flash—guarded treasure and held esoteric knowledge.

and wild birds; by fishing for cod, herring, salmon, and trout; and by wood carving, iron extraction, and rock quarrying. Raids, which usually took place during the summer months, gave way over three centuries to trade as a means of income generation. Trading towns were founded, from Kiev in Russia to York and Dublin in the British Isles. Although the farmers were generally self-reliant, iron, cooking utensils, whetstones, and steatite (soapstone) cooking pots were important export products and essential to the growth of trade.

Viking traders sailed to most parts of the known world, exchanging farm products, furs, and slaves for such valuables as gold, silk, silver, and weapons. Even in periods when Viking raids abounded, trade was conducted with western Europe. The Norwegian chieftain, Ottar, for example, visited King Alfred of Wessex as a peaceful trader at the same time that Alfred was waging war against other Viking chieftains. The southern Norway marketplace of Kaupang, near Larvik, was thriving then: Birka, near Malaren in Sweden, and Hedeby, at the German-Danish border, were boomtowns. Archaeologists digging at the sites of these now-deserted marketplaces have found Arab silver coins and Byzantine silk heaped together with the products of local blacksmiths, cobblers, and combmakers.

VERY FEW VIKINGS LIVED IN TOWNS. For the most part, they lived in one-story farmhouses with slanted roofs, often built close to the water from materials at hand. Builders made the walls mainly of wood or stone and covered the roof with shingles, sod, or straw. Turf houses, composed of stone foundations, turf walls, and thatched roofs, were common, especially in Iceland and Greenland. Viking houses had few or no windows. Each home included a hearth that provided heat and light as well as a place to cook. Raised platforms on either side of the hearth served as beds.

Three or more generations of a Viking family lived together, and the family was bound together by honor. If one member of the family was disgraced, the entire family, including its ancestors, was disgraced as well. Conflicts between individuals of different families often evolved into feuds between the families. The husband ruled the Viking family, but Viking women had more rights than did the women of other European societies of that time. For example, any Viking woman could own land or other property, and a wife had a right to share in the wealth that her husband gained. Viking law permitted a married woman to get a divorce whenever she wished, in some cases even getting her dowry back. Polygamy was sometimes practiced.

Most food, including beef, bread, cheese, eggs, and milk, came from the family farm. In Greenland, records indicate that polar bear and seal meat were sometimes served. Vikings ate with spoons and knives but no forks, although they used forks for cooking. They ate two meals a day, both of bread, vegetables, and meat. Large amounts of beer were consumed with the second meal but not the first.

Most Viking men wore two basic garments: trousers that reached to the knee or ankle and long-sleeved pullover shirts that reached below the waist. Viking women wore loose-fitting dresses of linen, covered with wool tunics that hung almost to the ankle. All the Vikings wore leather shoes.

Sports and games were usually contests of strength and endurance. Rowing, skiing, ice skating, swimming, and wrestling were popular. Vikings also enjoyed watching horse races and playing board games. In one game, *hnefatafl*, players moved pieces around the board to capture or protect a king. Bards called skalds often entertained by reciting poetry and telling stories; not surprisingly, favorite subjects included gods and battles.

The Scandinavians worked skillfully at many crafts, especially metalworking and wood carving, producing superb examples of advanced craftsmanship. They created beautiful bracelets, necklaces, pins, and other kinds of jewelry, often from silver. Green-glass-beaded necklaces were popular, and amber was treasured. Woodworkers decorated homes, ships, and wagons with elegant, detailed carvings of warriors and real and imaginary animals, twisted and braided together in tight asymmetric arabesques. The Viking ships themselves were richly ornamented, as were some of their holdings, from simple wooden utensils to spectacular weaponry.

Some of the most remarkable Viking crafts have been recovered at burial sites, such as the one at Oseberg. Even in a fearsome warrior's grave, peacetime articles—sickles, scythes, and hoes—have been found alongside weapons. A blacksmith would be buried with a hammer, anvil, tongs, and file. Coastal farmers, often buried in boats, were laid in graves with fishing equipment at hand. Women's graves were often loaded with jewelry, kitchen articles, and artifacts used in textile production.

THE NORSE, LIKE THE CELTS, believed in many gods. Building on Germanic myths, which tell of conflicts between gods and monsters, Viking cosmology reflects a strong interest in the creation, destruction, and ultimate re-creation of the world. The gods established order, law, riches, art, and wisdom in both the divine and human realms. Meanwhile, monsters and giants posed a constant threat to order,

✷ THE SAGA AGE ✦

HE PROSE LITERATURE OF MEDIEVAL ICELAND IS A GREAT WORLD treasure—elaborate, various, strange, profound," writes the novelist Jane Smiley, who finds that the sagas "concern such basic human dilemmas that for the most part they are readily accessible and seductive ... both intensely familiar and intensely strange."

One of the two Vinland Sagas, *The Saga of the Greenlanders*, tells about Freydis Eriksdottir, daughter to Erik the Red and half-sister to Leif Eriksson. Freydis, her husband, and other Vikings from Greenland and Iceland travel to Vinland, the North America settlement. Once there, they argue over who will live in Leif's longhouse, which makes Freydis furious. Eager to return to Greenland, she convinces the Icelanders to trade their large boat for her smaller one.

Then she tells her husband, Thorvard, quite a different story. "I went to the [Icelanders], to ask to purchase their ship," she recounts. "They reacted so angrily; they struck me and treated me very badly,... unless you avenge this I will divorce you!" Thorvard orders his men to question the offenders. "They went at once to the longhouse of the brothers, entered while those inside were still asleep and took them, tied them up and, once bound, led them outside." Freydis orders the men killed, then says, "Hand me an ax" and kills the Icelanders' women, too.

"It was clear that Freydis was highly pleased with what she had accomplished," reads a modern translation of the saga. "She spoke to her companions: 'If we are fortunate enough to make it back to Greenland,... I will have anyone who tells of these events killed. We will say that they remained behind here when we took our leave.'" In the spring, they return home, "sailing the ship into Eiriksfjord in early summer."

Safely home, Freydis "made sure all her companions were well rewarded," since she wished to have her misdeeds concealed, but "eventually word got out. In time it reached the ears of Leif, her brother, who thought the story a terrible one." Although Leif believes that he is not the one to dole out punishment, he predicts "that their descendants will not get on well in this world." And indeed "after that no one expected anything but evil from them."

Hermiodr
ridur hier
hestinu Sle
ipni:

Hermiodur til heliar reid. hana fa
en naustrondum. hvorge Slyekur he
ti Skaid. H leipti ad Dytis Kiaptinu
þo helia þarva heydi þan. hulin (v
tu daudan moeb. Hermiod ey hrædan
van hälp blasitahanan. Skmeb. ley
um XLVII Eddu Dæmi Sagou.

Balldr helui

The Queen of the Dead rebuffs a hero's appeal for his brother's life in this illustration for the *Snora Edda*.

Viking Varangian Guards of Byzantium left behind a runic inscription in the Hagia Sophia in Constantinople, now Istanbul. Foliate ornamentation, opposite, decorates an ax from Denmark.

seeking a return to chaos. Such tales seem to suit a vigorous, restless people accustomed to warfare, insecurity, and hard weather. And while by the end of the Viking age Christianity had generally replaced the heathen religion of the Nordic countries, remnants remained. Some Viking descendants still actively cling to certain pagan beliefs and practices.

Nordic paganism venerated a pantheon of warrior gods and giants, serpents and dragons, who each had power over their own domains. Odin, old, wise, and one-eyed, was the supreme Viking deity; he parallels Woden, the preeminent god of the Germanic tribes. Chief among all the Norse gods and goddesses, Odin was father to Thor and lived in Asgard, along with the Aesir (sky gods). Thor, the giant killer, was the god of the warriors, unmatched in strength. Ruler of the sky,

Thor was the god of thunder and lightning, and his hammer, Mjollnir, shattered whatever it struck. Nordic people still wear a reproduction of Thor's hammer today as an amulet of good luck. Wednesday was named in honor of Odin ("Woden's day"), while Thursday was named after Thor ("Thor's day"). Friday was named for Frigg, the wife of Odin.

Physically potent Frey was the god of agriculture and fertility. His seductive twin sister, Freyja, was the goddess of love and fertility. Frey ensured the success of a harvest, and Freyja blessed each marriage. Quick-witted and handsome Loki, the god of fire, was a trickster and a sorcerer, unreliable and distrusted by the other gods. His mythic misadventures often created great problems for the Norse gods, and he split his loyalty between the gods and the giants, adversaries and eventual destroyers of the gods of Asgard. In trying to please both, Loki often found himself in deep trouble. He was the ultimate trickster, using his cunning and magical powers matched by no one, neither human nor monster nor god. He could travel freely between the various Norse worlds and often accompanied Odin and Thor on their journeys and adventures throughout the universe. Loki was so wise and clever that the gods often sought his advice. Yet when they followed his plans, they always risked his tricking them into dangerous situations.

The legendary antics of Odin and Thor, Frey and Freyja, Loki and the giants, all took places in locations beyond human ken. But Vikings believed that if they died fighting, they would be escorted by the Valkyries, comely warrior goddesses, to a splendid hall in Asgard called Valhalla. There their great reward would be to fight all day and feast all night, sipping endless amounts of mead with the gods through eternity.

The Viking gods had human traits. Like their Greek counterparts on Olympus, they lived a raucous life, full of fighting, eating, and drinking. They were strong yet unpredictable, and at times ruthless in their disregard for human life. The gods also had to be appeased from time to time. In Uppsala, Sweden, nine human sacrifices were offered at a celebration held every nine years at a great shrine adjoined by a sacred grove. Every tree there was believed divine because generations of victims had died and rotted there.

Pagan Vikings typically believed that trees were magical and that forests were inhabited by earth spirits. The great ash tree Yggdrasil was the pillar around which the various

Norse worlds evolved. The mythical tree connected the nine worlds of Viking myth. Odin was said to have hung in agonizing voluntary sacrifice from this tree to gain power over the runes and win control of knowledge and learning. Yggdrasil had three main roots: One grew out of Niflheim and Hvergelmir, the seething cauldron in which life originated. Another—guarded by a giant and nourished by the Well of Knowledge— grew from Midgard, where humans lived and the gods made land, water, and heavens from a slain giant's body. The third root sprang from Asgard, where day and night raced chariots across the sky as wolves chased the sun and moon. A nimble squirrel ran up and down Yggdrasil's trunk, carrying messages between the eagle at the top and the serpent gnawing its roots. Four deer nibbled its leaves and the serpent Nidhogg chomped on its lowest root, and yet Yggdrasil remained endlessly renewed, a symbol of life itself.

Contact between the Vikings and European Christians led to the end— or at least the end of active practice—of the Norse religion. Fascination with Viking cosmology continues to this day, inspired by the great Icelandic sagas—composed long after the conversion to Christianity but containing memories of old beliefs and customs—and the Icelandic Poetic Edda, pre-Christian poems recorded in the 13th century by Snorri Sturluson.

By the mid-900s, the Rus had adopted many of the customs of the East Slavic peoples. About 988, the Rus prince Vladimir I destroyed all the symbols of the Viking religion in Kiev and made Christianity the official religion of the Rus. Over the next century, English and Saxon missionaries helped make Christianity the chief religion in Scandinavia. The Vikings slowly ceased their roving, relinquished their heathen beliefs, and receded in power and importance. The age of the Vikings had passed. In roughly 250 years, the Norsemen had transformed Europe, penetrated Asia, and explored America. Their military glories were nearly over. One decisive struggle remained: Clontarf, the battle for Ireland.

Built before 900 and excavated near Oslo a millennium later, the Gokstad ship, opposite, served as the burial vessel for a wealthy Viking man. Right, a rock wrapped in wood served as a Viking anchor.

Vikings left the still, protected waters of Norway's Sognefjords in the

North Sea to expand their reach into the Faroes, the Hebrides, and Ireland.

CLONTARF
The Great Battle for Ireland's Unity

*See! warp is stretched
For warriors' fall,
Lo! weft in loom
'Tis wet with blood;
Now fight foreboding,
'Neath friends' swift fingers,
Our grey woof waxeth
With war's alarms,
Our warp bloodred,
Our weft corseblue.*
—"THE WOOF OF WAR"
FROM *Njal's Saga (The Story of Burnt Njal)*

Ireland's Rock of Cashel, ancient seat of kings, was home to Brian Boru, the hero of Clontarf.

Bronze Celtic helmet, circa 150–50 B.C.

HE COMPLICATED CULTURAL EXCHANGE BETWEEN THE CELTS
and Vikings fashioned an intricate fabric of interdependencies and rivalries that seemed destined to fray. The battle song called "The Woof of War" comes from the greatest
of the Norse sagas, *Njal's Saga (The Story of Burnt Njal)*, an epic of Icelandic
literature composed in the 13th century. The saga describes a 50-year
blood feud that began in the 10th century.

"The Woof of War" uses language and imagery drawn from the craft of
weaving to describe a battle. The term woof (or weft) comes from the Old
English *wefen*, to weave, and refers to the threads drawn crosswise through
the warp, or the set of threads strung lengthwise on a loom. This battle
song, then, describes a battle as a giant loom: "Men's heads were the
weights, but men's entrails were the warp and weft, a sword was the shuttle, and the reels were arrows." Although this image was created by the
author of *Njal's Saga* to describe events around the Battle of Clontarf in
1014, it also conjures up the passionate impulses that first delivered the
Norsemen to the British Isles—and their furious influence upon arrival.

*As depicted in this elk-horn carving found at Sigtuna, Sweden, Vikings entered battle wearing
conical helmets of metal or leather, not horned helmets as in the popular stereotype.*

The golden age of Celtic Christian scholarship and missionary work may have produced such masterworks as the *Book of Kells,* but it also had a tragic downside: By the early ninth century, news of the wealth contained in Irish monasteries (not merely altar vessels and ecclesiastical ornaments, but also food reserves and captives to be traded as slaves) had spread north to the Vikings.

Viking raiders began by sacking Ireland's holiest places of Celtic worship. Over time, they went on to colonize all Ireland. Celtic and Viking cultures mixed, creating a marriage of families and economies, but in conflict the brute force of the Norse newcomers always prevailed. Sometimes they established towns of their own.

Of all the Viking settlements, Dublin in particular flourished. Founded in the mid-ninth century, the town was given the name *Dubh Linn* ("the black pool"). It soon became a a wealthy center of a kingdom

ABOVE: *A silver penny, one of the first issued by Sitruis Silkbeard, displays this Norse King of Dublin (spelled "Dyflin" on the coin) and founder of Christ Church Cathedral.*

LEFT: *Unearthed Norse timber pathways span a modern excavation near High Street in Dublin. Finds show that Vikings continued to reside in Ireland long after their defeat at the Battle of Clontarf.*

of Norse settlers, big enough to be a country. The Vikings founded other Irish cities as well—Cork, Limerick, Waterford, and Wexford—and smaller settlements and market towns. They intermarried and formed alliances with Irish noble families. Norse settlers even adopted Irish boys, some of whom became the vicious fighters known to the Irish as the *Gall-Gael* (Sons of Death). Though the Irish were ferocious warriors, following in the footsteps of their Celtic ancestors, their military obligations amounted to only three fortnights every three years. Settled Norsemen soon proved valuable mercenary warriors, hired into the service of feuding Irish kings.

At that time, Ireland teemed with warring tribal factions. More than a hundred rival Irish clans—perhaps closer to 200—were divided among five kingdoms: Ulster, Connaught, Meath, Munster, and Leinster. This political situation meant that the Celts were often so preoccupied by their

own insular squabbles and internecine battles, they could not unite to drive off the marauding and mostly unwelcome Vikings.

Despite their constant political maneuverings, tribes maintained a loose unity through a longstanding tradition: Whoever held the hill called Tara in Meath could claim to be *Árd-rí* (High King) of all Ireland. Perched on the Plain of Meath, Tara overlooks some of Europe's most fertile pastureland. It was worshiped by the Celts as an entrance to the otherworld. St. Patrick is believed to have come to Tara to stare down Irish paganism and challenge the power of the Druids. For five centuries mystical Tara had been held by Meath's Uí Néill (O'Neill) dynasty, but by the early 11th century the low sloping hill had been long abandoned, its earthworks overgrown and its significance purely symbolic. The high kingship had become merely a title of declining value as clan rivalries precluded nationhood and sapped defensive strength that could have been more usefully deployed against the Vikings. Every Irish ruler wanted more than he had and stopped at little to increase his wealth and power. When diplomacy failed, as it often did, Irish kings resorted to war, cattle-raiding, tribute-taking, hostage-holding, intermarriage, betrayal, and the maiming or blinding of rivals.

OPPOSITION TO THE NORSEMEN'S SUPREMACY simmered in the southwest. Brian Boru (or Boroimhe, pronounced bo-roo), the younger son of the ruling clan of northern Munster, was born in 941 and raised with tales of Celtic heroism and lessons of Christian scholarship. Such schooling must have given rise to his ambitions to reclaim Celtic lands from the Norse intruders, for as a young man Brian Boru became a guerrilla fighter against the Norsemen.

With his brother, Mathgamhain, who was Munster's king, Brian drove the Vikings from Limerick, north of Munster, in 968. When Mathgamhain was killed in 976, Boru was crowned king of Thomond. He then avenged his brother's death and became king of Munster in 979. Over the next two decades, Brian gained control over at least three-quarters of the island. He engaged in a lengthy war with the high king, Malachi (also known as Mael Sechnaill), who ruled from Meath, to the northeast near Dublin. In the long run Brian formed a short-lived alliance with Malachi and defeated an invading Danish Viking army at Glenmama, southwest of Dublin. Together they killed 7,000 enemies,

Excavations near Dublin's waterlogged Wood Quay and Fishamble Streets have uncovered Viking-age artifacts: jewelry, coins, carvings, and furnishings, some dating to the early ninth century.

sacked the city of Dublin, and ravaged the region of Leinster. They flushed out Mael Morda, Leinster's king, who had tried to escape them by hiding in a yew tree.

Ever on the go, in 1002 Brian broke his peace treaty with Malachi, the high king in Meath, and marched to the hill of Tara to demand that he either submit his crown or engage in battle. Malachi asked for a month's delay to muster an army, and Brian granted his request. According to the Irish tradition of fairness in war, in which Brian believed, acting with a sense of honor would bring greater glory in victory.

Ultimately Brian forced Meath's King Malachi to abdicate, and thus Brian Boru became the ruler of Tara and therefore the high king of Ireland. He further designated himself Emperor of the Gaels, a lofty title that reflected his wish to unite Celtic lands. He adopted as his primary goal the eradication of Vikings from Ireland—a nearly impossible task, since the Norsemen had assimilated and become integral to Ireland's economy. Nevertheless, through cunning and strength, Brian eventually forced Viking forces into a pitched battle in 1014.

Under Brian, Ireland nearly underwent a brief renaissance and nearly became a unified nation. He was renowned as a builder of forts; in fact, this may have been his most significant military legacy. He confirmed Armagh as Ireland's spiritual headquarters, supported schools and monasteries, ordered locals rulers and priests to record their histories, and built roads and bridges. To finance his ambitions, Brian depended on the revenues generated by the great Viking towns. To secure his hold, his daughter, Slaine, married Sigtrygg of Dublin, while Brian himself made a marriage of power, uniting with Sigtrygg's mother, Gormflaith, who was the sister of Mael Morda, the Leinster king so ignominiously flushed from hiding. A former wife of Malachi, Gormflaith was a duplicitous woman.

In 1012 Mael Morda rose in revolt against Brian. A year later he formed a coalition that included Sigtrygg and members of other Irish clans who were also envious of the high king. Brian led a series of raids in the vicinity of Dublin in order to recapture the city, intending to tie down any Irishmen who were inclined to join the Viking forces. At stake was not just the economic stronghold of Dublin, but also Brian's position and power as high king.

A siege in the autumn of 1013 was unsuccessful, as was an attack in March 1014, and Brian was left recruiting troops—including Norse mercenaries—throughout Ireland and Britain. In an indication of his vulnerable position, Brian again aligned himself with Malachi of Meath,

Life-size carved limestone figure of Janus, dating from the second century B.C., guarded a pre-Roman Celtic sanctuary north of Marseille, France.

whom he had forcefully succeeded as high king. Meanwhile, Mael Morda and Sigtrygg increased and fortified their own armies in preparation for continued warfare against Brian Boru.

On the eve of the Battle of Clontarf, the largest battle in Irish history, Brian was in his seventies. He was nearing the end of his life but also approaching his greatest glory. History would remember Brian as the founder of Ireland, the ruler who united the nation and saved it from the Norse. Culturally, the Battle of Clontarf has come to be remembered as a key event of a golden age. Historians would remember the battle as the beginning of the end for Norse expansion in Ireland. The Battle of Clontarf has come down in legend as one of the most picturesque battles of the medieval period, and all accounts agree that the combat was lengthy and hard-fought, the slaughter dreadful.

Perhaps even more than myth and religion, it is the brutal reality of warfare in the time of the Celts and Vikings that defines their age and captivates ours. Bloody and destructive though it may be, warfare is, as many scholars contend, a form of communication—a conversation, governed by rules of engagement and codes of conduct and guided by

He who rules Tara rules all of Ireland. For 500 years the Uí Néill kings held sway over

this storied hill in Meath, until Brian Boru claimed the high kingship for himself. ⊰⊱

ambitions and obligations. An instinct for warfare may be innate; the ambiguities that surround engagements of war are essential elements of humankind's most complicated conversation. One intense phrase of that conversation was spoken during the time of the conflicts between the Celts of Irelands and the Viking Norsemen.

> The ravens gnaw
> the necks of men.
> The warriors' blood spurts out,
> a wild battle is fought,
> minds are troubled, sides are pierced
> in warlike deeds.

As in these lines from *Táin Bó Cúalnge—The Cattle Raid of Cooley,* an epic from as early as the eighth century, considered Ireland's *Iliad*—Celtic warriors belonged to a fearsome tradition. Gallic fighters from antiquity wore loud tunics and checked cloaks, and draped themselves with jewelry. A warrior's long hair was bleached and stiffened with lime, and his mustache was bushy and unruly. He carried a dagger and sword at his side and clutched a spear and wooden shield. Warriors often went to battle naked, covered in tattoos and blue body paint, wearing only a torque, bracelets, and sandals. They hardly ever wore armor.

Celts typically charged into battle challenging opponents to single combat, hurling taunts and insults along the way. The Romans, in their earlier encounters with these exposed, wild-eyed warriors, were shocked and terrified. Not only were the men naked, they were howling and, it seemed, possessed by demons. One of their standard battle customs was to cut off the heads of slain enemies; another was to place a sword or spear-point between an enemy's teeth while accepting the unfortunate warrior's surrender. Although centuries had passed and Brian's warriors were more Irish than Celtic, these soldierly archetypes must have inspired their battle behavior.

Viking forces charged with equal furor. The cruelest and most feared of all Viking warriors was called a *berserker,* one of a lifelong fellowship of fighters whose name came from the bearskin outfits that they sometimes wore. In the throes of battle, berserkers were known to roll their eyes, foam at the mouth, bite their own shields, and unleash blood-curdling howls that terrified and weakened their opponents. In this frenzied state, they raged into battle, sometimes naked and always appearing more like rabid, irrational wild animals than men at war.

After the defeat of the Norsemen at Clontarf, Brian Boru paused for grateful prayer. His moment of gratitude was interrupted when he was discovered, then decapitated, by the vengeful Viking Brodir.

Berserkers were in some ways the ultimate Vikings—and in other ways pariahs in their own society. They were respected as superb warriors but resented for their tendencies to turn indiscriminately on friends while their madness was upon them. Outside their official wartime role, the *berserkergang* were stock saga villains and murderous brutes, according to one scholar "a predatory group of brawlers and killers who disrupted the

peace of the Viking community repeatedly." They ransacked communities, including their own, slaughtered cattle, burned houses to the ground, and carried off wives and daughters. These excesses eventually led to the berserkers' demise. Along with *hólmgang*—a duel to the death considered a magical alternative to the parliamentary settling of disputes—the berserkergang was outlawed in 1015. But in the Battle of Clontarf, which took place on April 23, 1014, the berserkers played their battlefield roles to perfection.

CLONTARF IS LOCATED north of the River Liffey on the outskirts of present-day Dublin. Its name is derived from a compound word composed of *cluain* and *tarbb*, which combine to mean "the bulls' meadow." On this level plain, Brian and Malachi met the forces of Leinster and the Norse.

The day before the battle was a busy one, filled with machinations and deceptions. As Brian amassed troops and laid plans to attack Dublin, he received two pieces of news, one good, another bad. First the bad: the Irishmen of Meath, followers of Malachi, refused to take part in his battle plans. They may have been mulling over old quarrels. While not unexpected, the resignation was troubling. But then Brian received word that the Viking forces had boarded their longships and headed out to sea, apparently deserting Sigtrygg's battle chief, Sigurd, and departing from Ireland.

In fact, the whole scene was actually a clever ploy to catch the Irish off guard, for as soon as the Norse longships were out of the sight of land, they turned back and started sailing toward Dublin. The Vikings came ashore on the strand north of Dublin, between the city and the army of the Irish, and spent the night sharpening their blades. What's more, the Norsemen seemed to have the gods on their side: Sigtrygg's primary ally, Sigurd, was carrying a sacred banner, woven by his mother. It featured the image of a raven—a sign of Odin, Norse god of war. The banner had magical properties that would ensure victory—but also promise death—to the army that carried it.

As dawn broke, the Norsemen assembled on the shores near Clontarf. Nearby lay their beached boats, a mile and a half from the city walls of Dublin. Brian's chiefs persuaded him to take no active part in the battle, but he remained a force behind the Irish lines. And though reluctant to take part in a battle on Good Friday, he did ride before his assembling forces, carrying a crucifix in one hand and a sword in the other. He gave a short but inspiring speech to his warriors assembled to do battle and then retired to the rear, accompanied by a number of personal guards who formed a shield all around him.

On the front line, both armies adopted a shield-wall formation and pressed in toward one another. One history of the battle describes Brian as he looked out upon a sea of his advancing warriors "and beheld the battle phalanx, compact, huge, disciplined, moving in

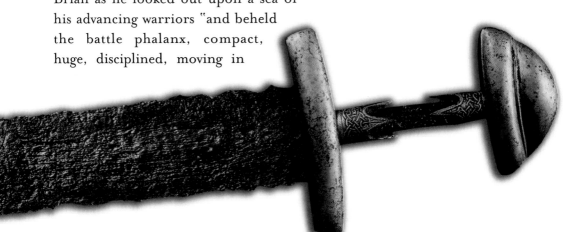

Hammered bronze and red glass decorate the Battersea Shield, opposite, found in the Thames River. Irish copper-hilted iron sword, above, must have struck lethal blows against many a Viking marauder.

Some wealthy Viking warriors wore elaborate chain-mail tunics. They carried heavy wooden shields to protect against the blades, spears, and arrows of their Celtic foes.

silence, mutely, bravely, haughtily, unitedly, with one mind, traversing the plain towards them; and three score and ten banners over them, of red, and of yellow, and of green, and of all kinds of colors." The warriors carried shining spears and battle axes, protective shields and swords "for hewing and for hacking, for maiming and mutilating skins, and bodies, and skulls."

It's doubtful if Brian's army appreciated the political issues at stake. More likely they set out singing marching songs, excited by the opportunities for the glory and plunder that battle always provided. Their weaponry was probably identical to that of the Vikings in this epic confrontation. Most fought with a sling, club, dagger, spear, axe, or sword and shield. Despite Brian's efforts to introduce a type of cavalry,

Irish warriors still fought on foot—barefoot. Irish chiefs employed kerns—lightly armed skirmishers who used javelins, even though such longer-ranged missile weapons were considered a less-than-honorable method of inflicting casualties. Chiefs from both sides wore chain mail and helmets and wielded heavy two-handed battle axes, yet a fundamental inequality existed between the battle garb of the Irish and the Norse. The vast majority of Brian's warriors wore simple tunics with woolen cloaks or shaggy mantles; some had body protection in the form of boiled leather fitted to the torso or an occasional set of chain links taken from a dead Viking. The Norse, on the other hand, were encased from head to foot in metal, according to one history of the conflict. The lack of such armor among the Irish troops was a great and foreboding disadvantage.

THE BATTLE BEGAN IN AGE-OLD HEROIC TRADITION. Numerous leaders called one another out to meet in single combats meant to settle old grudges and garner personal fame and glory. As clan feuds were settled and years of animosity between the Norse and the Irish boiled over, the fighting grew more and more fierce. One Viking chief roared across the field to an Irish leader, "Where's Domhnall?" A reply came swiftly: "Here, thou reptile." Soon each man fell, gripping the other's hair in hand, the other's sword in breast. Such was the tone of the grim, no-quarter combat at Clontarf.

Double-edged swords, often with richly ornamented hilts decorated in gold or silver, were Viking warriors' weapons of choice.

✦ VIKINGS in ✦ BATTLE

The War-Crazed "Berserkers"

HE ENGLISH WORD "BERSERK" COMES FROM THE NAME for the fellowship of fighters whose frenzied battlefield behavior secured Viking victories time after time.

Some historians believe that the berserkers were raging madmen. Others think they were adrenaline-junkie warriors who became wild and fearless by eating hallucinogenic mushrooms, drinking huge amounts of mead (honey wine), mastering breathing techniques that evoked a state of fearless distraction, or chanting magic incantations. However they achieved their war-crazy state, the berserkers entered a frenzy that made them immune from pain.

"A man who went berserk was seized by a battle-madness far beyond courage," writes historian David Howarth. "He killed and killed, without mercy, reason or fear, and did not stop until there was nobody left to kill, or until he fell dead himself."

Berserkers are often described as being fantastically ugly, sometimes mistaken for trolls. This could be a way to describe the strength of the savage warrior, known to drink the blood of a bear or wolf and complete the metamorphosis by assuming a battle name containing the words *bjorn* (bear) or *ulf* (wolf). Because he could change into bestial form, or at least assume the ferocious qualities of a beast, the berserker is associated with the All-father Odin, who could shape-shift into a bird, fish, or wild animal. This connection to Odin secured berserkers an important role in royal armies, since the Norse believed Odin to be god of kings and protector of royal power. In their rage, berserkers attacked boulders and trees. Sometimes they even killed their own people.

After a warrior attained the state of *berserkergang*, he often experienced complete physical disability, as described in *Egil's Saga:* "It is said that people who could take on the character of animals, or went berserk, became so strong in this state that no one was a match for them, but also that just after it wore off they were left weaker than usual. Kveldulf [one such hero] was rendered completely powerless and had to lie down and rest."

Walrus-ivory chess piece depicts a frenzied Viking berserker, ready to rush madly into battle, murdering with wild abandon. Devotees of Odin, berserkers may have achieved a state of wide-eyed battle readiness by self-hypnosis or by ingesting hallucinogenic mushrooms.

MASSED ONLOOKERS CHEERED. Individual contests were fought between old enemies. As the two armies slowly began to crash into each other, combat intensified. Vikings pounded the Irish center. Some of the heaviest and most brutal fighting took place in thick woods, where it is said "the trees dripped with the blood of the slain." An evocative description of the battle comes from the 12th-century history *Cogadh Gaedhel re Gallaibh (The War of the Irish with the Foreigners)*, which calls the battle "the clashing of two bodies of equal hardness, and of two bodies moving in contrary directions in one place. And it is not easy to imagine what to liken it to; but to nothing small could be likened the firm, stern, sudden thunder-motion, and the stout, valiant, haughty, billow roll of these people on both sides."

There were heavy losses all around as the battle raged for most of the day. One account describes "wrestling, wounding, [and a struggle] noisy, bloody, crimsoned, terrible, fierce, quarrelsome." The initial crush saw the Vikings and rebel Irish drive back their enemy with the men of Leinster slaughtering their rivals from Munster in droves.

Sigurd battled fiercely and watched the prophecies of his magical raven banner come to pass. One of Brian's warriors led a ferocious attack directed at the raven standard and viciously killed the Vikings near it, slaying the standard-bearer and his replacement. Soon no one was left who would dare bear the standard. When Sigurd ordered the chieftain Thorstein to pick it up, he refused, as did Hrafn the Red, who said "Bear thine own devil thyself." So Sigurd himself took up the banner marked with the raven and fearfully hid it under his cloak. But the power of the raven's spell quickly overwhelmed such a timid deception. In no time at all, Sigurd suffered the same fate as the previous standard-bearers: He was slain by the spear of Brian's son Murchad.

Without a leader and with the tide turning in favor of Brian's Irish, the Viking line began to waver. Bloody bodies were all around, and the will of the rapidly shrinking enemy force finally broke. Only when the Norse Army began fleeing back to Dublin did Malachi and the Irishmen of Meath enter the battle fray. They decimated the retreating Vikings, who were caught between the Irish and the sea. The beaches in front of the ships were already lost, and many men who attempted to swim to the ships farther offshore drowned. Warriors retreated to the sea, according to a chronicle, "like a herd of cows in heat, from sun, and from gadflies, and from insects."

A few small bands, however, were cut off by the advancing Irish and scattered in all directions. One of these ragged battle divisions ended up fleeing past the Irish encampment, where they came across King Brian. In his harried, battle-weary form, the Viking warrior Brodir burst through the thinned pen of shields, lifted to guard the high king as he prayed. The Viking hero struck him down with an ax, decapitating the old king while boasting, "Now let man tell man that Brodir felled Brian!" But Brodir's bloody victory was short-lived. He was instantly captured and immediately sentenced to death by being tied to a tree with his own intestines.

Thus the epic battle ended, at monumental cost. True, the Norse and Leinster armies were annihilated; every one of their leaders was slain. From an army of 6,600, only 600 survived. But the Irish paid dearly for their victory, with the death of Brian, his son Murchad, his grandson Tordhelbach, his brother Cuduiligh, and his nephew Coniang, together with 1,600 other nobles and 2,400 warriors. Brian's army began the day 7,000 men strong; at the end, fewer than 3,000 survived. The body of Brian—whose head, according to folklore, magically reattached itself—was carried to Armagh and buried beside the cathedral he had restored there. A plaque on the modern cathedral now standing at the site identifies the great Celtic Irish hero's resting place.

MEDIEVAL RECORDS CLAIM it as a brilliant victory, but the battle of Clontarf proved a mixed blessing for the Irish. High King Brian Boru had been slain. His troops eventually held the field, but they were decimated to such an extent that they could do no more than march home. They left untouched the Viking stronghold of Dublin, whose capture had been their goal. There was no longer any clear line of succession. Malachi once again declared himself high king, and few resisted him. And although the Norse were now considered subjects of the Irish high king, Sigtrygg, Brian's son-in-law, who had watched the battle from Dublin and was permitted to live, ended up reigning for another 22 years. If Brian had been younger when he won at Clontarf, and if he had lived to exploit his victory, he would have punished the kingdom of Leinster, which by opposing Brian sought to destroy his vision of a unified Ireland. As it stood, the victory at Clontarf was hollow: Brian had not completely driven out the Vikings, nor had he succeeded in unifying his land. The Vikings remained a presence in Ireland.

But the Battle of Clontarf did play a major part in ending the power of the Vikings. As a result of Brian's victory, the iron grip of the Vikings began to wane. Over the next 50 years, pushed farther back toward their homelands in Norway and Denmark, the Vikings concentrated further battle efforts in England and Scotland instead. In fact, just two years

after the Battle of Clontarf, a Danish Viking called Canute became the king of England.

Clontarf still remains a tale of national struggle in Irish folklore, the first (and arguably the greatest) battle ever fought for the unity of Ireland. Stories, songs, and poems of glory and battlefield prowess at Clontarf appeared over the next few hundred years, and they took on singular importance even after the Normans invaded and conquered Ireland in the 1170s. It was said that any Irish family who could not claim an ancestor killed at the Battle of Clontarf could not be considered truly noble.

They sang victory songs, yet a century of disorder followed, not nation-building. Clontarf marks a moment in Irish history when the possibility of nationhood gave way to petty rivalry.

UPON HIS DEATH, High King Brian Boru was almost immediately cast in

With drinking horn in hand, opposite, legendary maidens known as Valkyries welcomed dead warriors to Valhalla, above, Odin's hall of heroes, where they feasted for eternity.

the role of an Irish national hero and defender of the Christian faith. He left behind an ideal of national unity evoked ever since, whenever the cause of Irish nationalism seeks its historical roots. For the Irish, he was a mystical leader, just as Arthur was for the Britons.

Such hagiography, however, can be carefully cultivated. As history proves, the world's great leaders frequently play a dominant role in the creation and documentation of their own achievements. In life Brian nurtured his heroic identity and generated political support through lavish liturgical patronage and political cunning. A scholar and perceptive student of history, he required his monastical minions to record the story of Ireland with patriotic flourish, up to and including his own grand accomplishments as high king. It is in part because of this effort that the Battle of Clontarf has been handed down in the sagas and the chronicles not as a domestic squabble but as an epic struggle of Christian Ireland against vicious pagans. This portrayal was conveniently heightened by the facts that the battle occurred on Good Friday and that High King Brian was killed while at prayer, thanking God for victory.

From our vantage point, a period of legend and pseudo-history followed Brian's death. The saga *Cogadh Gaedhel re Gallaibh,* written during this time, is exclusively devoted to the invasions of the Vikings and the reaction of the Irish; it details Brian's campaigns from 968 to 1014, culminating in the Battle of Clontarf. A partisan document, it casts Irish King Brian in the role of martyred savior while portraying the Viking position as avaricious barbarianism—even though many Vikings fought on Brian's side. It also exaggerates the significance of the Battle of Clontarf itself, which was really one stage in a much longer, drawn-out dispute over the distribution of Ireland's limited wealth.

Dynastic propaganda or not, *Cogadh Gaedhel re Gallaibh* is a genuine medieval page-turner that colorfully describes the miseries that the Vikings are alleged to have inflicted on Ireland. One segment describes waves of heathen Vikings descending on Ireland's shores and swimming

up waterways such as the Boyne, Liffey, and Shannon Rivers, determined to plunder Ireland at her heart:

> *Immense floods and countless sea-vomitings of ships and boats and fleets so that*
> *there was not a harbor nor a land-port nor a dun nor a fastness in all Mumhan*
> *[Munster] without floods of Danes and pirates . . . so that they made spoil-land*
> *and sword-land and conquered land of her, throughout her breadth and generally;*
> *and they ravaged her chieftainries and her privileged churches and her sanctuaries;*
> *and they rent her shrines and her reliquaries and her books.*

Unlike Ireland's monastic annals, which emanated from ecclesiastical circles and highlighted the plundering of monasteries, sagas such as *Cogadh Gaedhel re Gallaibh* were commissioned by Irish royal dynasties in order to enhance their claims to kingship. *Cogadh* was compiled on behalf of Brian Boru's descendants and depicts Brian as the savior of Ireland. As its title suggests, the tract was intended to imply a united Irish opposition to the Norsemen. Other medieval histories, like the *Annals of Ulster*, merely amplify the generalizations levied by ninth-century authors, such as one who calls

ABOVE: *Irish kings collected hostages in warfare, secured them in iron collars like this, and offered them as a tribute guarantee.*

LEFT: *On the Gundestrup Cauldron, a silver bowl found in Denmark, soldiers and trumpeters march by as the Celtic god Teutates performs a human sacrifice.*

the Vikings "wild beasts" who go "by horse and foot through hills and fields, forests, open plains and villages, killing babies, children, young men, old men, fathers, sons and mothers.... They overthrow, they despoil, they destroy, they burn, they ravage, sinister cohort, fatal phalanx, cruel host."

IN THE MANIPULATIONS OF RECORDED HISTORY, Vikings were more than just sinister characters conceived by the Irish imagination. The Norsemen actively and artfully documented their plunderings, battles, successes, and failures in the sagas, their own idealized versions of their history. The great Norse sagas often chronicle events now considered history. *Njal's Saga (The Story of Burnt Njal)*, the 13th-century Icelandic epic, describes events that likely occurred between 930 and 1020, including the period of Christian conversion in 1000.

Njal's Saga describes the obligations of bloodlines and portrays ordinary people who are confronted with violence. It tells of Icelanders crossing the North Sea to Scandinavia, men who leave their native land to seek fortune elsewhere, and men slain on points of principle. It also narrates

Stone circles mark noblemen's final resting places in Scandinavia's

largest burial site, Lindeholm Hoje, in Jutland, Denmark. ✠

Discrete form meets deadly function in Viking battle attire, Spartan in its simplicity.
This conical headgear is the only complete Viking-age helmet ever found.

the story of a queen who curses a marriage. Sorcery and violence are stitched into this epic account of the destruction—through ritual burning—of the saintly hero named Njal and his family. The story is made compelling by the interweaving of fiction and fact, and the locations are both in and outside of Iceland.

An important episode comes at the end of the saga, as action shifts south to the Orkneys, the Irish Sea, and Ireland, and the narrative becomes a Viking account of the events precipitating and including the Battle of Clontarf. *Njal's Saga* provides the battle's most extensive account in any work composed outside Ireland, although some information about Clontarf can be found in other Icelandic tales, including *Thorstein's Saga, Orkneyinga Saga,* and a lost work called *Bjarn's Saga.*

Apart from their divergent nationalistic and literary stylings, *Cogadh Gaedhel re Gallaibh* and *Njal's Saga* agree on certain aspects of Clontarf. First, they both portray Brian's scheming wife, Gormflaith, as responsible for starting the chain of events that led to the battle. Second, both epics describe how both sides divided their armies into three groups or battle lines for conflict, and both point out how that division is significant for understanding the outcome of the encounter. Third, according to both the Irish and the Viking version, after the Vikings were in retreat, fleeing to the river, they found their ships floating in mid-channel, forcing them to stand their ground or swim and risk drowning. Finally, both sagas offer elaborate descriptions of Brodir slaying Brian.

Njal's Saga does not attempt to color Clontarf as anything but a Viking disaster, yet in an epilogue it lists the supernatural manifestations that occurred during the battle, a passage that succeeds in framing the defeated Viking warriors as noble and heroic even in defeat. After the battle, a man named Daurrud heads to a bower and peeps through a slit to see a dozen women chanting a song of destruction while they work at a loom made of swords, arrows, human heads, and intestines.

> *This woof is y-woven*
> *With entrails of men,*
> *This warp is hardweighted*
> *With heads of the slain,*
> *Spears blood-besprinkled*
> *For spindles we use,*
> *Our loom ironbound,*
> *And arrows our reels;*
> *With swords for our shuttles*
> *This war-woof we work;*
> *So weave we, weird sisters,*
> *Our warwinning woof.*
>
> *...*
>
> *Wind we, wind swiftly*
> *Our warwinning woof.*
> *When sword-bearing rovers*

The eighth-century Ardagh Chalice, found in Ireland's County Limerick in 1868,
is made of silver and bronze, ornamented with gold filigree, blue and red glass, and rock crystal.

> To banners rush on,
> Mind, maidens, we spare not
> One life in the fray!
> We corse-choosing sisters
> Have charge of the slain.
> ...
> Now bare we our brands,
> Now haste we hard, maidens,
> Hence far, far, away.

The weavers suggest that although the Irish were victors at Clontarf, the heroic Vikings will live to fight again on Earth and into time eternal, achieving the immortality they so fiercely sought.

THE CHAPTER WRITTEN about the Battle of Clontarf in *Njal's Saga* ends when word that the Norsemen have been defeated by the Irish makes its way swiftly back to Iceland. A song, heard by an earl during a dream, turns out to be a short summary of the battle and a blunt description of its outcome:

> *I have been where warriors wrestled,*
> *High in Erin sang the sword,*
> *Boss to boss met many bucklers,*
> *Steel rung sharp on rattling helm;*
> *I can tell of all their struggle;*
> *Sigurd fell in flight of spears;*
> *Brian fell, but kept his kingdom*
> *Ere he lost one drop of blood.*

Clontarf marked the beginning of the end of Viking domination in Ireland, but the struggle for control of the British Isles raged on in England. There, countless bloody battles would yet be fought, thousands of lives lost, and more than a few legends written before the Norsemen would finally retreat to their homelands and cease their roaming. The Viking vanquishment from Ireland may have presaged their eventual drubbing in England—but before that could happen, the Danes would achieve power and wealth beyond measure and for a time become the dominant force in northern Europe.

Gold, silver, copper, glass, enamel, and amber,
the eighth-century Tara Brooch displays animal
ornamentation and sophisticated geometric
patterns arising from druidic
astronomy and math.

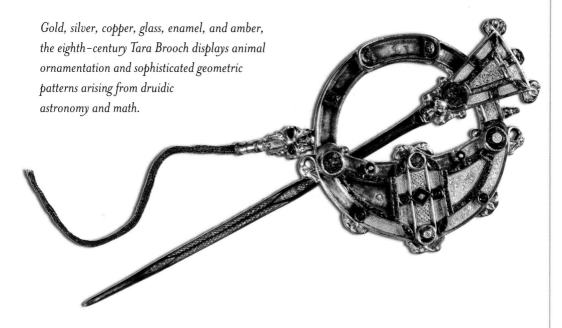

⊹ THE CELTS ⊱
in BATTLE

The "Warp-Spasm" of a Hero

RELAND'S GREATEST LEGEND *TÁIN BÓ CÚALNGE*, OR *THE CATTLE RAID of Cooley*, is the central epic of the Ulster Cycle, one of the four cycles of Irish mythology. It tells of the mighty Cú Chulainn, the bravest warrior in first-century Ireland and the model mythical champion of Gael.

A son of Lugh, the Celtic god of light, Cú Chulainn possessed supernatural powers that helped him defend his land and people. The story begins with Ailill and Maeve, king and queen of Ireland's provinces, arguing over who has the most impressive belongings. Their possessions are equal in all arenas except that Maeve's best cow, a powerful and ferocious white-horned bull, has joined Ailill's herd. To match her husband, Maeve conspires to gain possession of the most famous bull in Ireland, the brown bull of Cooley, owned by an Ulster chieftain. She asks to borrow the brown bull for a year but is rebuffed, so Queen Maeve declares war. To her early advantage, an old curse still keeps the men of Ulster from defending themselves. Only 17-year-old Cú Chulainn has escaped the curse, making this young fighter Ulster's sole defender.

By tradition, passionate Irish heroes became possessed when confronted by the enemy, and their appearances could alter considerably, through a phenomenon they called the "warp-spasm"—not unlike the battle-madness experienced by the Viking berserkers. So when the armies of Connacht confront Ulster's Cú Chulainn, he appears as "a monstrous thing, hideous and shapeless, unheard of. His shanks and his joints, every knuckle and angle and organ from head to foot, shook like a tree in the flood or a reed in the stream. His body made a furious twist inside his skin, so that his feet and shins and knees switched to the rear and his heels and calves switched to the front."

His face turned even more monstrous and frightening, as "he sucked one eye so deep into his head that a wild crane couldn't probe it onto his cheek out of the depths of his skull" while "the other eye fell out along his cheek." His cheeks peeled back from his mouth, revealing his gullet; his internal organs flapped in his mouth and throat. The fury of the gods seemed embodied in the Ulster warrior as "malignant mists and spurts of fire—the torches of Badb [the crow, a war goddess]—flickered red in the vaporous clouds that rose boiling above his head, so fierce was his fury." A "hero-halo" rose around his brow and a tall spout of black blood rose up out of his skull. He was terrifying and invincible.

In spine-tingling defense of his people, Cú Chulainn unleashes hell on Maeve's army, leaving bloody heads spiked on tree branches. It was said that some of Maeve's shellshocked warriors perished at the sight of him. Eventually the Ulstermen rise up and join Cú Chulainn, forcing Maeve's men into retreat. Along the way, Maeve seizes the brown bull of Cooley, which escapes, kills the white-horned bull, and wreaks havoc all across Ireland until it falls dead of exhaustion.

Cú Chulainn's heroic victory has its cost. Seven years later a vindictive Maeve leads an army back to Ulster. Warriors whose fathers had been killed by Cú Chulainn ask a sorcerer to fashion magical spears that can kill a king.

Cú Chulainn mounts his chariot alone, disregarding omens of doom. Maeve's evil henchmen land a spear in his side. The hero light above the head of Ulster's champion begins to fade, and then his enemies move in closer and slice off the great warrior's head.

Roman sources and recent archaeological finds suggest that some Celts battled naked, wearing only torques and blue body paint.

❈ Brian Boru's son Murchad (left) sets his eyes on the Danish standard

at the Battle of Clontarf, fought near Dublin on Good Friday in 1014. ⊹

CHAPTER 5

IMMORTALITY ACHIEVED

The Legacy of the Celts and Vikings

She told me once to carry
My head always high in battle
Where swords seek to shatter
The skulls of doomed warriors.

—The last poem of Harald Hardraada, King of Norway (r. 1046–1066)

Celtic crosses such as this one in a County Wicklow cemetery have come to symbolize Ireland.

Silver-gilt thistle brooch, circa tenth century A.D.

ONG BEFORE THE BATTLE OF CLONTARF IN 1014, THE Vikings renewed their raids on England, meeting head-on the increasing strength and unity of the Anglo Saxons. In 1013 the Danes launched a full-force invasion of England, marched on London, drove out Anglo-Saxon King Ethelred, and captured the city. Ethelred returned with Olaf of Norway and took back London, yet by the early 11th century the Danes controlled the whole of England and Normandy, plus trade in the Baltic. How did the Vikings transform from a loosely affiliated coalition of warlike bands to the dominant force in England? Defeat upon defeat, it turns out, wisened the Norsemen, forcing them to develop organizational and diplomatic skills that equaled their proven mastery of the battle ax.

While many stories of Viking raids celebrate the terrifying efficiency, the Norsemen weren't always successful. Sometimes they were even slaughtered on arrival by local defense forces well-prepared for attack. At other times large Viking armies were outmaneuvered and overpowered by a superior leader, such as Alfred, King of Wessex, who constructed

This fortress in Fyrkat, Denmark, housed the troops of King Canute, ruler of Denmark and Norway, who launched a full-scale invasion of England in 1015.

Coins, brooches, ingots, and arm rings comprise the Cuerdale Hoard, largest Viking treasure found in the British Isles. A Norseman stashed all in a lead chest beside the River Ribble around 905 A.D.

massive warships and fortresses and eventually drove out the Danes and defeated the Vikings in 878. In 886, Alfred captured London and began uniting the Anglo Saxons under the Wessex dynasty, aiming to be king of England. He struck a treaty with Guthrum to create the Danelaw, the vast area of England that followed Danish law and customs. Peace did not last long. Between 899 and 924, Alfred's son, Edward the Elder, continued the struggle, defeated the Danes, and advanced into East Anglia, Essex, and central England. His successor, Ethelstan, established an alliance with Eric Bloodaxe, the fierce Viking leader of Northumbria, the last Viking area of England. Following Ethelstan's death in 939, rival factions fought for several years to gain control of Wessex. Eric Bloodaxe was killed in 964 and England united for the first time under Edred.

The Vikings were relentless, though, and another series of violent raids hit English shores in 980. England eventually protected itself by paying off the invaders through Danegeld (Dane's Gold), a tax first levied in 865 and used to buy off raiding Danes. By 980, Danegeld had become a regular tax, employed dramatically in 991 after the Battle of Maldon, when the Scandinavians were bought off with ten tons of silver. Such a suicidal policy bought peace in the short term but depleted the coffers and encouraged invaders to strike again. The Danes returned in 1002 to collect another ten tons of silver, and England's ineffectual King Ethelred II—not "unready," as some mistakenly call him, but *unraede*, ill-advised—found himself unable to purchase security and fearful of conspiracy and revolution. In response, he had hundreds of Danish settlers living in England murdered.

A disastrous time for England followed, with deadly Viking invasions between 1003 and 1006. In 1010 the Danes burned Oxford, Ipswich, and Cambridge. In 1014 they tore down London Bridge on the Thames, inspiring the song "London Bridge is Falling Down." Danegeld mounted, and the Vikings took an estimated 70 tons of silver. Ethelred fled to Normandy, and the Danes—first under Svein and later under Canute the Great, who became king in 1016—consolidated Viking control over Norway, Denmark, and England. Over the course of his long rule, Canute restored the church to high place, codified English law, and even married Ethelred's Norman widow, Emma. Her homeland in Normandy presents an interesting picture of the interaction of Celtic and Viking cultures.

BEFORE JULIUS CAEASAR CONQUERED IT, Normandy was part of ancient Celtic Gaul. Christianized in the third century, conquered by the Franks in the fifth century, and repeatedly devastated in the ninth century by the Vikings, it was finally ceded by Charles III (Charles the Simple) in 911 to the Normans' chief, Rollo, who became the first duke of Normandy. The Norsemen—or Normans, for whom the region was named—adopted Christianity in the tenth century, and the customs and language of France. They abandoned piracy and dedicated their energies to commerce and European trade.

The turbulent period of Danish rule in England had two endings. The first was with the crowning of Edward the Confessor in 1042. Son of King Ethelred II and Emma, and stepson of Canute, Edward caused unrest by awarding lands and titles to Norman barons over their English counter-parts. The pious Edward ruled England in a time of complex allegiances both international and interfamilial. He left no heir when he died in 1066. William, Duke of Normandy, cited a longstanding promise of inheritance, while the Saxon Harold Godwinson insisted that the dying Edward bequeath the throne to him.

Harold was pronounced king, but the crown of England was still hotly contested by challenges from the north and from Normandy. The harassed King Harold did not rule England long, but long enough to realize the second and final outcome of Viking involvement in England. On September 25, 1066, the powerful forces of King Harold defeated the Norwegian invaders at Stamford Bridge in Yorkshire, killing the last great Viking hero, Harald Hardraada (a cognomen that means "hard ruler"), King of Norway. Harald the Ruthless, as he was called, had been a Varangian guard in Byzantium. He was a poet and traveler who had journeyed to Jerusalem, a legendary adventurer who waged constant battle against the Danes and Normans. At his death—from an arrow in the throat—Viking power in the British Isles was forever extinguished.

Two days after the death of Harald the Ruthless, William, Duke of Normandy, set sail for England. William was a descendent of Rollo, the Viking warrior whose army had overrun Normandy just one century before. Deep within William, though a Norman baron, simmered the unquenchable Viking thirst for battlefield glory. That he found on October 14 at the Battle of Hastings. He became William the Conqueror by engineering the defeat of the English troops and the death of King Harold of England, killed by an arrow through the windpipe. On Christmas Day 1066, with the Norman Conquest secured, William was crowned king. He became one of England's greatest monarchs and a pivotal ruler in European history.

PERHAPS THE MOST ASTONISHING RELIC OF THIS AGE—and certainly the longest—is the Bayeux Tapestry, a narrow strip of embroidered linen stretching about 230 feet that records the Battle of Hastings and the events leading up to it. A lingering tradition suggests that the tapestry was embroidered by Queen Matilda, wife of William the Conqueror, although its date may be later. It depicts Viking longships, helmets, coats of mail, shields, and weapons such as lances, swords, and axes. In one scene two soldiers carry a heavy shirt of copper and iron mail on a pole threaded through its sleeves. In other scenes men cart provisions to boats

The Venerable Bede, an Anglo-Saxon Benedictine monk, was history's first scholar to document hand gestures for numbers, which he did in his work on the ecclesiastical calendar.

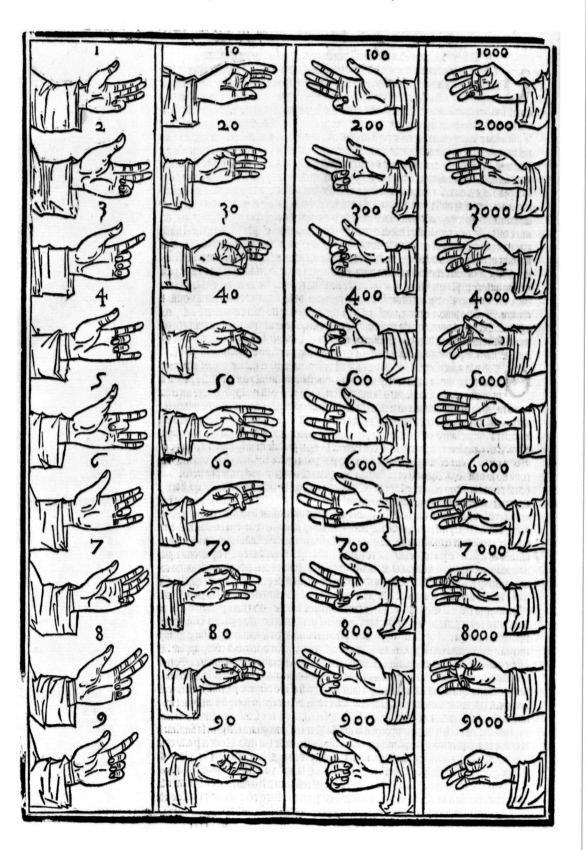

ABOVE: *Since 1308 almost every English monarch has been crowned on this chair, designed to enclose the famous Stone of Scone.*

RIGHT: *Westminster Abbey, as shown in this 19th-century painting, stands at the site where Ethelbert, King of Kent, built a church in the early seventh century.*

already loaded with men and horses, preparing to cross the English Channel. While the Bayeux Tapestry provides fascinating clues to the art of warfare in the late Viking age, other extant material evidences the Norse sea wolves' indomitable Viking spirit: from masterful steel weaponry to magical silver jewelry, from intricately carved longships to eternal sagas, from runes carved on a balustrade at the Hagia Sophia in Istanbul to ruins in L'Anse aux Meadows, Newfoundland.

Travel to Viking homelands today—Sweden, Denmark, Norway, Iceland—or Viking-settled lands such as England, and the ancient legacy comes alive in museums and research centers. The Jorvik Viking Center in York, England, details the history of a site where an unprecedented number of Viking-age objects have been excavated. The center stages a vibrant Viking festival every February. In Iceland, history buffs can join in the

annual June Viking Festival at the Viking Village in Hafnarfjörður, where locals and visitors feast like Thor while learning about Viking customs. In the capital, Reykjavik, medieval vellum saga and edda manuscripts are displayed at the Culture House (*þjóðmenningarhúsið*), a vault of priceless works from pagan times through the Viking expansion, the settlement of the Atlantic Islands, and the Christianization of these northern peoples.

Among the most spectacular living vessels of the Vikings are Norway's ancient stave churches. These towering wooden Christian churches display elegant mythological and ornamental motifs such as dragon heads and vine tendrils. Some of these pine-built churches have survived for 900 years. Sweden's Sigurd Rock displays a fascinating set of Viking-era carvings as well. The Viking Ship Museum (Vikingskiphuset) in Oslo, Norway, contains countless relics as well as magnificent oak ships

Scenes in the Bayeux Tapestry depict Normans in chain mail, charging

into the Battle of Hastings and forcing the overpowered English to flee.

unearthed from Norse burial mounds. In the 1960s the remains of five Viking ships dating from the 11th century were discovered at Skuldelev in the Roskilde Fjord, Denmark—a find that revealed an enormous amount of new information about the techniques of Viking shipbuilding. Similar discoveries continue to this day, each revealing more about Viking life.

Some discoveries literally shimmer. The Cuerdale Hoard, uncovered in Lancashire, England, in 1840, is the greatest Viking silver treasure trove ever found outside Russia, far greater than any found in Scandinavia or in the western areas of Viking settlement. From the early tenth century, it included 8,600 items, all silver coin and bullion. The treasure may have been buried for security, for religious reasons—sacrificed to the gods or stashed for the afterlife—or simply as an elaborate ceremony. Weighing 325 grams, the biggest Viking gold arm ring ever found in the British Isles was discovered in 2004 among the belongings of a York man. Each year brings new finds. Helmets, armor, weaponry, tools, jewelry, silver, coins, dwelling places, rune stones, burial remains, and even toys help tell the story of the Vikings.

THE GREATEST VIKING LEGACY, however, is not material but conceptual. In A.D. 930 chieftain-priests gathered at the rocky breach of Thingvellir, a visible portion of the Mid-Atlantic Ridge. There they proclaimed laws and settled disputes, giving birth to the idea of democracy in Iceland, and probably the world. Their gathering, called the Althing, is an ancestor of today's parliament, and it helped establish the belief that by law all men are created equal—even though Viking society was rigidly divided into classes.

Henry II, Norman king of England, crossed the Irish Sea in 1171 to assert his mastery over Ireland during the chaos following the death of Brian Boru.

In a similar way, the literature of medieval Iceland is a great world treasure, on a par with the works of Homer and Shakespeare. Viking sagas stand as the archetype of the modern novel. The vital force behind these timeless

Henry II issued Dublin's first municipal charter, declaring the city his colonial capital.
In the cathedral atop the Rock of Cashel he accepted a pledge of fealty from Irish bishops.

tales, conveyed orally before being written down in the 12th and 13th centuries, is the elaborate, precise, and colorful Old Norse language. Its best-known words still with us today are those beginning with *sk*, such as "sky," "skill," and "skin." Words concerning the law (from the Old Norse *lagu*), such as the word "wrong," come from the Old Norse, showing the influence of the Danelaw system. Everyday words such as "get," "take," "window," "die," "egg," "bread," "husband," "fellow," "happy," "ill," and "muck" all originate from Viking words spoken in England, where trading and farming, then intermarriage and assimilation helped create a melting pot of Old Norse and Old English. Historians determine the spread of Viking settlements by analyzing place-names for telltale linguistic roots.

Celt and Viking tribal names show up in modern places. The Boii gave us Bohemia; the Belgae settled Belgium; the Helvetii made their home in Switzerland; the Treveri in Trier; the Parisii in Paris; the Redones in Rennes; the Dumnonii in Devon; the Cantiaci in Kent. Wherever the Celts migrated, from Portugal to Poland, their tribal names made themselves at home. An ability—if not always a willingness—to merge culturally is a trait shared by both Vikings and Celts. As the first Indo-European people to spread across Europe, the Celts reached the Black Sea and Asia Minor, Spain, Italy, and the British Isles. They carried their language from south-central Europe in the fifth century B.C. has been called proto-Celtic; it developed into other continental Celtic dialects. The Greeks called the Celts in the Balkans and Asia Minor Galatae, and the Galatian language remained in use until the fourth century A.D. The Celts were known as the Celtiberi in Spain, where inscriptions in Celtiberian have been found. The first wave of Celtic invasions into the British Isles in the fourth century B.C. led to the Goidelic branch of the Celtic language; the second to the Brythonic. Respectively, they evolved into Irish, Scottish Gaelic, and Manx; Welsh, Cornish, and Breton.

On at least two memorable modern occasions, Celtic languages spread outside Britain. First, in the early 19th century, many Gaels emigrated to Cape Breton Island in Nova Scotia, leading to the development of the Cape Breton Gaelic dialect. Then in 1865, 150 Welsh successfully established a settlement in Argentina's Patagonia. Today a few thousand of their descendants speak Patagonian Welsh as well as Spanish.

NOWHERE IS THE LEGACY of the ancient Celtic language more cherished than in Wales, a peninsula on the western flank of England where Cymraeg—the language of the people—can still be heard in pubs and markets. Street signs and train posters proudly spell out Welsh instructions and place-names. "Wales is not the smallest of Europe's minority nations, with some 2.9 million people, but its history is among the most complex," writes Jan Morris in *A Writer's House in Wales*. "Almost everything about it, in fact, is convoluted—long-winded, its critics might say—and its self-esteem is considerable." North Wales claims one of the world's longest place-names: Llanfairpwllgwyngyllgogerychwyrndrobwyllllantysiliogogogoch.

Written Welsh first appeared in the eighth century A.D., making it one of the oldest languages in Europe today. It is also the world's most actively spoken Celtic language, but its competition is rather anemic. Fewer than 400,000 people speak Welsh, representing half of all speakers of non-English or non-French languages in all Celtic lands. It is anticipated that over the next two decades, the Breton language will become extinct, and the world total of speakers of Celtic languages will drop to half a million. This situation leaves the cultural legacy as well as those who promote it in something of a quandary. "All the Celtic revivals of the past and present have been predicated on the existence, somewhere, of people for whom these languages, traditions, and beliefs actually mean something," writes Marcus Tanner.

*Dragon–headed finials inspired by Norse mythology decorate this Scandinavian stave church
in Norway, symbolizing a blend of Viking and Christian sensibilities.*

Shown on this embossed and gilded plate from Denmark, King Harold Bluetooth renounced paganism, embraced Christianity, and experienced holy baptism around 960.

IN HIS BOOK, *The Last of the Celts*, Marcus Tanner asks whether there will be a lasting Celtic renaissance. As he started to answer the question, the sounds of Celtic revivals were ringing in his ears. "There is nothing that the British or the French love more than a good old Celtic revival. The British, French, and North American public who know any-thing of the subject have been lulled into believing a Celtic renaissance is going on.... [But] this new-baked Celticism owes almost nothing to the traditional culture of Ireland, the Scottish Highlands, Wales or Brittany. It is a marketing device."

Celtic revivals, Tanner explains, were always the work of outsiders. They reflected the need among the English and French for contracting otherness and have little connection to the actual life and beliefs of true Celtic soci-eties. The image of Celtic saints as superhuman heroes practiced in magic and dragon-slaying comes from later chroniclers and mythologizers.

Many early Celtic revivalists were monks who hoped to attribute the foundation of their monasteries to saints representing a lost golden age. St. Patrick is a good example: After being virtually forgotten for two cen-turies following his death, he was rediscovered during a Celtic revival that started in the 690s and quickly transformed him from a fallible human to the fantastic, serpent-expelling supernatural being venerated annually on St. Patrick's Day. Columba, the sixth-century Irish missionary who founded Iona, underwent a similar transformation, in which this visionary founder of monasteries became a saintly magician who could make stones float, raise people from the dead, change water to wine, and drive a monster from a stream—miracles familiar to readers of the Old and New Testaments.

The good will of Celtic revivalists even extended to the Anglo-Saxons, who in the fifth and sixth centuries had driven the Britons to their remote new lands. The Northumbrian historian called the Venerable Bede was a monk who died in 735. Author of the *Ecclesiastical History of the English People*, he was one of the first Englishmen to romanticize Ireland as a land of saints and scholars. A second Celtic revival followed the Norman Conquest of 1066, then 12th-century historian Geoffrey of Monmouth created the elaborate King Arthur tales, honoring this Celtic British hero who had kept the Anglo-Saxons at bay. Additional Celtic revivals followed in the Reformation and Romantic periods.

In the 1890s, the idea of a Celtic commonwealth uniting Ireland, Scotland, and Wales gained popularity. The Gaelic League sought to revive the Irish language and endowed the Celtic Gaels with moral and spiritual superiority over the materialistic English. A Celtic congress followed, then civil war in Ireland. Celtic nationalists had to come to terms with the increas-ing anglicization of Ireland. Poets and writers grappled with the distinction and bridged the gap between the idealized Celtic Ireland of the past and the self-defining Ireland of modern times. The poems of William Butler Yeats, Austin Clarke, Patrick Kavanagh, and Thomas Kinsella are rich with social

Old Vikings never die: The annual Up Helly Aa festival at Lerwick in the Shetland Islands

culminates in a ceremonial conflagration, burning a replica of a Norse longship. ✳

❊ J.R.R. TOLKIEN ❊

Celtic and Viking Influences on Middle-earth

F CERTAIN CELTIC AND VIKING MYTHS AND IMAGES SEEM strangely familiar—even uncannily cinematic—it might be because they markedly influenced the recent blockbuster *Lord of the Rings* films. Celtic and Viking aesthetics helped create the intricate settings for the epic struggle waged over the realm called Middle-earth. In the films—and, more importantly, in the books that inspired them—large-footed, cheery creatures called hobbits overcome demonic forces by joining in a heroic fellowship with elves, trolls, and men. Wizards, talking and walking trees, ghost warriors, vile wraiths, a fiery eye in the sky, and a schizophrenic, greedy, smelly, amphibious, cave-dwelling, raw fish—eating trickster populate some of the most imaginative pages ever written.

J. R. R. Tolkien was an Oxford professor of Anglo-Saxon language and literature. Chief among the myths that inspired his fiction was the epic poem *Beowulf,* a blend of historical events and Nordic legend likely composed in the seventh or eighth century and spread primarily through song or spoken verse before being written down around A.D. 1000. *Beowulf* tells the adventures of a Scandinavian hero, Beowulf, who saves the Danes from the seemingly invincible monster Grendel and then from Grendel's even more gruesome mother. Beowulf finally returns to his own country, where he perishes in a vivid fight against a dragon. Other mythological foundations that influenced Tolkien include Iceland's Poetic Edda, from which names of the dwarves in his book *The Hobbit* were derived; the *Kalevala,* a 19th-century compilation of ballads and poems that serves as the Finnish national epic; Norse mythology, including one tale in which Odin owns an all-powerful ring; and England's late 14th-century Arthurian epic, *Sir Gawain and the Green Knight.*

Tolkien studied philology, the branch of linguistics concerned with the ancestry of languages, and was literate in Latin, French, German, Welsh, Finnish, Old English, and Old Norse. He invented "faerie languages" such as Elvish (including Quenya, reminiscent of Finnish, and Sindarin, reminiscent of Welsh), Dwarvish, and Entish, the language of the trees. The names of many of the characters and places in his books are derived

from antique languages. The term "hobbit" comes from *hol bytla,* Old English for "hole-dweller." Middle-earth, the battleground between the forces of good and evil, is related to *middan-geard,* "Earth" in Old English poetry. The Dark Lord Sauron is linked to the Old Norse or Icelandic stem meaning "filth," "dung," or "uncleanness." The name of his evil realm, Mordor, derives from the Old English word for murder. "The invention of languages," Tolkien wrote, "is the foundation. The 'stories' were made rather to provide a world for the languages than the reverse."

Tolkien created the mythology and history of Middle-earth to serve as the poetic legend he felt England lacked. He mourned the loss of oral histories and the legends of the Romans, Angles, Saxons, and Jutes, then the Danish and Norwegian Vikings, and finally the Normans arriving in 1066. Each new influence ineffably altered England's imaginative landscape. Tolkien's despair over the loss of these contributing cultures and languages resonates throughout his great works, *The Hobbit,* published in 1936, and *The Lord of the Rings* trilogy, published in 1954 and 1955.

J. R. R. Tolkien, best known in his lifetime as an Oxford professor, is now better known as the inventor of Middle-earth and the author of of the Celt-inspired trilogy, Lord of the Rings.

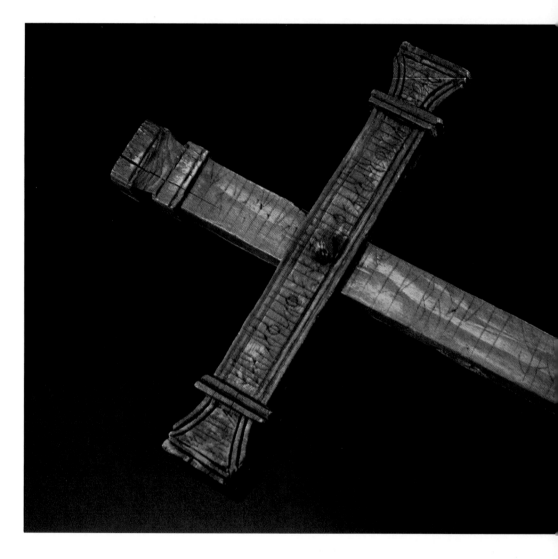

and political aspects of Celtic-infused Irishness. James Joyce's landmark 1922 novel *Ulysses* is a modernist masterpiece that employs Celtic lyricism and vulgarity to describe with extraordinary sensuality and vibrancy one ordinary day in Dublin 1904.

In 1866, decades before Joyce documented Dublin's nooks and crannies, the British poet and literary critic Matthew Arnold delivered a landmark address at Oxford University. He reflected on the "genius" of Celtic literature and culture and advocated the thorough study of the "Celt and things Celtic" at Oxford. "Wales, where the past still lives, where every place has its tradition, every name its poetry, and where the people, the genuine people, still knows [*sic*] this past, this tradition, this poetry, and lives with it, and clings to it," he wrote. "I regard the Welsh literature—or rather, dropping the distinction between Welsh and Irish,

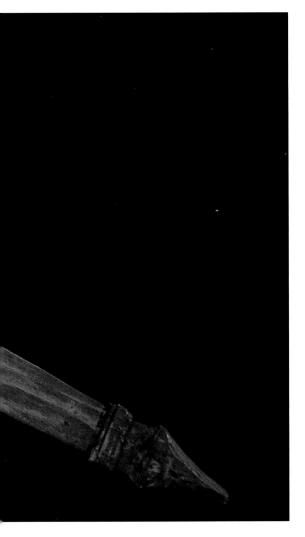

ABOVE: *Indefatigable missionary and most beloved of Ireland's holy men, St. Patrick is credited with Christianizing vast areas of the island—and ridding it of snakes.*

LEFT: *Runic inscriptions decorate this ten-inch wooden cross, discovered at a settlement in Greenland.*

Gaels and Cymris, let me say Celtic literature—as an object of very great interest." Yet Arnold still upheld the standard Victorian English proposition that the perpetuation of the Celtic language—in Wales in particular—was an abomination that his Saxon "brothers" of the British Isles simply could not abide.

"The fusion of all the inhabitants of these islands into one homogeneous, English-speaking whole, the breaking down of barriers between us, the swallowing up of separate provincial nationalities, is a consummation to which the natural course of things irresistibly tends; it is a necessity of what is called modern civilisation, and modern civilisation is a real, legitimate force; the change must come, and its accomplishment is a mere affair of time," believed Arnold. "The sooner the Welsh language disappears as an instrument of the practical, political, social life of Wales, the better; the better for England, the better for Wales itself." Arnold celebrated the artistic accomplishments of the Celts but he blamed their marginalization as a people on their poetical, dreamy, sensual, essentially feminine character—a community character that valued love and beauty, charm and spirituality over practicality and cold, calculated effectiveness.

EACH AGE CHOOSES THE MYTHOLOGY that best suits its current ideology. Until Queen Victoria, the English portrayed Vikings as bloodthirsty and violent. But during the 19th century, interest in Viking myth and lore peaked. Public perceptions changed, and the furious Norsemen turned from pagan barbarians to civilized exemplars of respectable values: bold, brave, poetic, virtuous, democratic, innovative, upwardly social, and eager to convert to Christianity. Such virtues mirrored those at the heart of British nationhood, writes Andrew Wawn, a professor of Anglo-Icelandic Studies at the University of Leeds: "Victorian enthusiasts regarded old northern pagan piety as preferable to modern scientific rationalism." The 19th-century composer Richard Wagner wrote operas based on Viking legends, including *The Valkyrie,* customarily cast with full-figured, blonde-haired warrior women wearing horned helmets and elaborate cross-gartering as the mythical maidens of Valhalla. Today, Viking images help promote both the agendas of a professional football franchise in Minnesota and a line of pricey stoves.

Nor have the Celts escaped modern references. One of the most common symbols of this timeless civilization is the Celtic cross—a cross enclosed in a circle or nimbus, pagan in origin and predating Christianity by centuries. The icon is often found in American cemeteries, often embellished with intricate tracery. Archaeologists have long depicted the Celts as a brave and poetic tribal people, not unduly aggressive, who battled their way across Europe and managed to kept ethnic unity alive across a huge span of territory and time. Certainly with this reputation in mind, a professional basketball team in Boston chose to extend the venerable Celtic brand name into a new arena.

"The ancient Celts bequeathed more than language, literature, and works of art to European civilization," writes art historian Miklos Szabo. "They gave it the heritage of a sensitivity and an intellectual disposition which, down the centuries, remains the protagonist in a continuing dialogue with the various manifestations of the classical tradition."

The magical incantations of Amergein, one of Ireland's earliest poets, provide a mystical conclusion to this chronicle of the Celts' desire to explore the realms of intellectual speculation. The poet suggests that communion with nature has made him blissfully one with the universe, peaceful in spirit, and great in mind.

> *I am the wind which blows over the sea,*
> *I am wave of the sea,*
> *I am lowing of the sea,*
> *I am the bull of seven battles,*
> *I am bird of prey on the cliff-face,*
> *I am sunbeam,*
> *I am skilful sailor,*
> *I am a cruel boar,*
> *I am lake in the valley,*
> *I am word of knowledge,*
> *I am a sharp sword threatening an army,*
> *I am the god who gives fire to the head,*
> *I am he who casts light between the mountains,*
> *I am he who foretells the ages of the moon,*
> *I am he who teaches where the sun sets.*

A similar conclusion befitting the tales of fearsome Vikings and their furious sea dragons is harder to come by. The sagas describe a culture that stands on virtues of strength, honor, exploration, and constructive interaction—but the historical record favors depictions of ghastly raids and blinding violence. The Vikings themselves were sometimes complicit in emphasizing their brutal pagan heritage, if only to make their refinements that much more impressive. The *Knútsdrápa,* an 11th-century poem written in praise of Canute, the Danish king of England, contains the following archetypally Viking allusion:

> *And Ívarr,*
> *Who dwelt at York,*
> *Carved the eagle*
> *On Ælla's back.*

Any Viking-fearing reader would immediately recognize the allusion. It refers to the blood-eagle, a horrifying yet apocryphal means of torture. It may be an ignominious thing to be remembered for, but it does suit the plundering Norsemen, the lords of the seas and lightning raiders. In this and in so many other ways, the Vikings made their mark.

Brought by Vikings to this rugged North Atlantic island, small and woolly

Icelandic ponies are renowned for their gentle demeanor and smooth gait. ✦

AUTHOR'S NOTE

YEARS AGO I FOUND MYSELF WANDERING MIDDLE-EARTH—or at least a place that felt like Middle-earth—and my thoughts turned to Vikings. I was in Iceland, on a road trip from Reykjavik, and my first destination was Thingvellir National Park, site of a chiseled rent in the landscape that marks one of Earth's most visible examples of plate tectonic theory. That doesn't sound like it has much to do with the bloodthirsty Norsemen of saga lore, or even with the brave Icelandic seafarers who defined their age, but it does. Thingvellir is a shallow canyon that resembles an endless Earth-hewn zipper. Underneath this rocky gash—technically speaking, the Mid-Atlantic Ridge—two tectonic plates, the North Atlantic and the Eurasian, violently pull apart under the pressure of raging thermodynamic torrents, forcing Iceland to expand outward by about six and a half feet a century. Within this chasm Iceland's Althing, a rudimentary parliament that presaged modern democracy, first convened in A.D. 930. When you walk around and within this crevasse two sensations powerfully emerge: First, awe—awe that a culture could forge an existence on these churning plains, and not just survive, but triumph over adversity for more than a thousand years. And second, fear—a brief flash of frightful envy that there once was (and Icelanders say still is) a community of weather-beaten pagan heroes who for two centuries dominated coastal, and great stretches of continental, Europe before striking out across the Atlantic to reach North America 500 years before Columbus landed. It's astonishing.

This book aims to place the achievements and legacies of two of Europe's defining cultures in historical context. Covering more than a thousand years of European social evolution, it is not a comprehensive account of the Celtic and Viking culture. The richness of these civilizations runs far deeper than this simple account. Fortunately, a number of excellent resources are available for further study. To the authors of the works listed here as well as many others, I am grateful for their focus and insight, which helped form the foundation of this book.

This book is dedicated to my friends, my favorite Celts, MacIntosh, MacGregor, and Abercrombie Stone, and to lovely Sophia.

I express gratitude to my brilliant editors Johnna Rizzo and Susan Tyler Hitchcock, and to the crackerjack National Geographic Book Division staff that labored to make this volume look so good, especially art director Melissa Farris and photo editor Paula Soderlund. Thanks also to Barbara Brownell Grogan, Dale-Marie Herring, and researcher Jane Sunderland. And I especially appreciate the support, insights, and affection of my friends: P. F. Kluge and Pamela Hollie, Jill Muffy Pollack, Kyeh Kim, Grant Wiggins, Matt Voorhees, Chris Dorobek, Brett House, Elizabeth Midgley, Giles and Meredith Roblyer, Shannon Wilkinson, Dave Bouman, the Men of 2717 (Peter Bepler, Brian Feintech, Jason Lott, John Russell, Jed Sundwall, Tim Valentiner), Stone Scholar Gregg Helvey, primatologist McKenzie Funk, Julian Smith, Geoffrey Saunders Schramm, Ryan Towell, Malcolm Auchincloss, Tina Purohit, Valerie Hletko, Susan O'Keefe, Norie Quintos, Heather Morgan, Jerry Sealy, Jayne Wise, Sheila Buckmaster, Nandita Khanna, Dan Westergren, Marilyn Terrell, Paul Martin, Keith Bellows, Pat McGeehan, Nichole Shea, Lora Price, Suzanne King, Eric Ofori Asamoah, Jessica Buckholz, Ann Loeffler, Roa Lynn and Bernard Kripkee, Ryan Towell, Erik Tallroth, Lisa Johansson, Magnus Lindelow, Stephanie Kuttner, Malcolm Ehrenpreis, Elizabeth Littlefield, Nancy Kwon, Stephan Danninger, Wendy and Joe Van Dyke-Lupton, Harry Schechter and Misha Keefe, Yooh-Yung Kim, lion hunter Stuart Wheeler, Marrett Taylor, Steve Loomis, Deborah Laycock, Perry Lentz, Jack Finefrock, Phil Church.

With love and gratitude to Spencer and Prudy, Christy and Spencer Jr. (Bub), and Paige (Niblet) Stone, grandparents George R. and Viola H. White, Ellen Decker Stone, and Ruskin Beechler, and Lorraine Stone, Papa Abe and Muzzy Steinberg, Diane, Erwin, Andy and Stacy Bernstein.

— George W. Stone

INDEX

Boldface references indicate illustrations.

ACKROYD, PETER. *London: The Biography.* Nan A. Talese/ Doubleday, New York, 2000.

ALLEN, TONY. *The Vikings: The Battle at the End of Time.* Duncan Baird Publishers, London, 2002.

BENGTSSON, FRANS GUNNER. *The Long Ships: A Saga of the Viking Age* (titled *Red Orm* in Swedish). Trans. Michael Meyer. HarperCollins, New York, 1984.

BIEL, JÖRG. "Treasure from a Celtic Tomb." NATIONAL GEOGRAPHIC, March 1980.

BRIDGEFORD, ANDREW. *1066: The Hidden History in the Bayeux Tapestry.* Walker & Co., New York, 2005.

CAHILL, THOMAS. *How the Irish Saved Civilization.* Nan A. Talese/Doubleday, New York, 1995.

CAHILL, THOMAS. *Sailing the Wine-Dark Sea: Why the Greeks Matter.* Nan A. Talese/ Doubleday, New York, 2003.

CHANCE, JANE. *Tolkien's Art: A Mythology for England.* University Press of Kentucky, Lexington, KY, 2001.

COHAT, YVES. *The Vikings: Lords of the Seas.* Harry N. Abrams, New York, 1992.

CUNLIFFE, BARRY. *The Celtic World.* McGraw-Hill, New York, 1979.

CUNLIFFE, BARRY. *The Extraordinary Voyage of Pytheas the Greek.* Penguin Books, New York, 2002

DAVIES, NORMAN. *Europe: A History.* Oxford University Press, Oxford & New York, 1996.

GRIFFITHS, TONY. *Scandinavia: At War with Trolls—A Modern History from the Napoleonic Era to the Third Millenium.* Palgrave

Macmillan, London, 2004.

HARPUR, JAMES. *The Atlas of Sacred Places.* Henry Holt & Co., New York, 1994.

HAYWOOD, JOHN. *The Penguin Historical Atlas of the Vikings.* Penguin, New York, 1995.

HOWARTH, DAVID. *1066: The Year of the Conquest.* Viking, New York, 1978.

HUBERT, HENRI, RAYMOND LANTIER, MARRYAT R. DOBIE, AND HENRI BERR. *The Rise of the Celts.* Dover Publications, New York. 2002 (original edition, 1934).

HUDSON, BENJAMIN. "Bjarn's Saga," *Medium Aevum,* 71: 2. Society for the Study of Medieval Languages and Literature, Oxford, 2002.

JONES, GWYN. *A History of the Vikings.* Oxford University Press, Oxford & London, 2001.

JORDAN, ROBERT PAUL. "When the Vikings Sailed East." NATIONAL GEOGRAPHIC, March 1985.

KEISTER, DOUGLAS. *Stories in Stone: A Field Guide to Cemetery Symbolism and Iconography.* Gibbs Smith, Layton, Utah, 2004.

LA FAY, HOWARD. *The Vikings.* National Geographic Society, Washington, D.C., 1972.

LINDEN, EUGENE. "The Vikings: A Memorable Visit to America." *Smithsonian Magazine,* December 2004.

MAGNUSSON, MAGNUS. *Vikings!* E. P. Dutton, New York, 1980.

MAGNUSSON, MAGNUS. *Viking Expansion Westwards.* Henry Z. Walck, New York, 1973.

MAN, JOHN. *Atlas of the Year 1000.* Harvard University Press, Cambridge, 1999.

MARKALE, JEAN. *Celtic*

Civilization. Gordon & Cremonesi, Paris, 1976.

MARKALE, JEAN. *Merlin: Priest of Nature.* Inner Traditions, Rochester, Vt., 1995.

MOFFAT, ALISTAIR. *Before Scotland: The Story of Scotland Before History.* Thames & Hudson, New York, 2005.

MORRIS, JAN. *A Writer's House in Wales.* National Geographic Society, Washington, D.C., 2002.

NATIONAL GEOGRAPHIC SOCIETY. *Beyond the Movie: Lord of the Rings.* http://www.national geographic.com/ngbeyond/ rings/. 2003.

OBREGÓN, MAURICIO. *Beyond the Edge of the Sea: Sailing with Jason and the Argonauts, Ulysses, the Vikings, and Other Explorers of the Ancient World.* Random House, New York, 2001.

Peoples and Places of the Past, National Geographic Society, Washington, D.C., 1983.

ROBERTS, J. M. *A History of Europe.* Allen Lane/The Penguin Press, New York, 1996.

ROBINSON, ANDREW. *The Story of Writing.* Thames & Hudson, London, 1995.

ROESDAHL, ELSE. *The Vikings.* Penguin, New York, 1999.

ROSS, ANNE. *A Traveller's Guide to Celtic Britain.* Routledge & Kegan Paul, London, 1985.

RUTHERFURD, EDWARD. *Sarum.* Arrow Books, London, 1987.

SAWYER, P. H. *The Age of the Vikings.* St. Martin's Press, New York, 1971.

SAWYER, PETER, ED. *The Oxford History of the Vikings.* Oxford University Press, Oxford & London, 2001.

SEVERY, MERLE. "The Celts." NATIONAL GEOGRAPHIC, May 1977.

SMITH, PATRICK. J. "Violence, Society and Communication: the Vikings and Pattern of Violence in England and Ireland 793-860." School of History, University of Leeds, UK. www.leeds.ac.uk/history/e-journal/Smith.pdf/.

TANNER, MARCUS. The Last of the Celts. Yale University Press, New Haven, Conn., 2004.

THORSSON, ÖRNÓLFUR, ed. The Sagas of Icelanders, especially the Vinland Sagas: The Saga of the Greenlanders (Grænlendinga saga) and Eirik the Red's Saga (Eiríks saga rauða). Transl. Keneva Kunz. Viking, New York, 1997.

VESILIND, PRIIT J. "In Search of Vikings." NATIONAL GEOGRAPHIC, May 2000.

VILLIERS, CAPT. ALAN, et al. Men, Ships, and the Sea. National Geographic Society, Washington, D.C., 1973.

Walks Through Britain's History. W. W. Norton, New York and London, 2001.

WAWN, ANDREW. "The Viking Revival." British Broadcasting Company, 2001. http://www.bbc.co.uk/history/ancient/vikings/

WEBB, JAMES. Born Fighting: How the Scots-Irish Shaped America. Broadway Books, New York, 2004.

WOOD, JULIETTE. The Celtic Book of Living and Dying. Sterling Publishing Co., New York, 2000.

WOOD, JULIETTE. The Celts: Life, Myth, and Art. Stewart, Tabori & Chang, New York, 1998.

FROM MIST AND STONE

By George W. Stone

Published by the National Geographic Society

John M. Fahey, Jr., *President and Chief Executive Officer*

Gilbert M. Grosvenor, *Chairman of the Board*

Nina D. Hoffman, *Executive Vice President*

Prepared by the Book Division

Kevin Mulroy, *Senior Vice President and Publisher*

Kristin Hanneman, *Illustrations Director*

Marianne R. Koszorus, *Design Director*

Barbara Brownell Grogan, *Executive Editor*

Staff for this Book

Susan Tyler Hitchcock, *Editor*

Melissa Farris, *Art Director*

Paula Soderlund, *Illustrations Editor*

Jane Sunderland, *Researcher*

Rebecca Barnes, *Contributing Editor*

Margo Browning, *Contributing Editor*

Johnna Rizzo, *Contributing Editor*

Carl Mehler, *Director of Maps*

Nicholas P. Rosenbach, *Map Researcher and Editor*

Gregory Ugiansky, *Map Production*

Meredith Wilcox, *Illustrations Specialist*

R. Gary Colbert, *Production Director*

Richard S. Wain, *Production Project Manager*

Cataldo Perrone, *Design Assistant*

Manufacturing and Quality Control

Christopher A. Liedel, *Chief Financial Officer*

Phillip L. Schlosser, *Managing Director*

John T. Dunn, *Technical Director*

Chris Brown, *Manager*

One of the world's largest nonprofit scientific and educational organizations, the National Geographic Society was founded in 1888 "for the increase and diffusion of geographic knowledge." Fulfilling this mission, the Society educates and inspires millions every day through its magazines, books, television programs, videos, maps and atlases, research grants, the National Geographic Bee, teacher workshops, and innovative classroom materials. The Society is supported through membership dues, charitable gifts, and income from the sale of its educational products. This support is vital to National Geographic's mission to increase global understanding and promote conservation of our planet through exploration, research, and education.

For more information, please call 1-800-NGS-LINE (647-5463) or write to the following address:

National Geographic Society
1145 17th Street N.W.
Washington, D.C. 20036-4688 U.S.A.

Visit the Society's Web site at www.nationalgeographic.com.

Library of Congress Cataloging-in-Publication Data
Stone, George W.
  From mist and stone: the folklore of the Celts and Vikings / George W. Stone. p. cm.
  Includes index.
  ISBN 0-7922-3817-6
  1. Celts--History. 2. Civilization, Celtic. 3. Vikings--History. 4. Civilization, Viking. I. National Geographic Society (U.S.)II. Title.
 D70.S76 2005
 936'.004916--dc22
 2005050541